RUSSIA 1914–41
FOR CCEA AS LEVEL

Jim McBride

COLOURPOINT
EDUCATIONAL

Jim McBride has been an
A level teacher for over
thirty years as well as being
a senior examiner. He is an
expert on Russian history
and a member of the
EUROCLIO team developing
resources on modern
Russian history.

Throughout his career
Jim has been involved in
curriculum development
and in producing support
material for teachers and
students. He is secretary
of the History Teachers'
Association of Northern
Ireland.

COLOURPOINT
EDUCATIONAL

Colourpoint Educational
An imprint of Colourpoint Creative Ltd
Colourpoint House
Jubilee Business Park
21 Jubilee Road
Newtownards
County Down
Northern Ireland
BT23 4YH

Tel: 028 9182 6339
Fax: 028 9182 1900
E-mail: sales@colourpoint.co.uk
Website: www.colourpoint.co.uk

Contents

Publisher's Note

This book has been written to help students preparing for 'AS 2 Option 5: Russia 1914–41' of the History specification from CCEA. While Colourpoint Educational and the author have taken every care in its production, we are not able to guarantee that the book is completely error-free. Additionally, while the book has been written to closely match the CCEA specification, it is the responsibility of each candidate to satisfy themselves that they have fully met the requirements of the CCEA specification prior to sitting an exam set by that body. For this reason, and because specifications change with time, we strongly advise every candidate to avail of a qualified teacher and to check the content of the most recent specification for themselves prior to the exam. Colourpoint Educational therefore cannot be held responsible for any errors or omissions in this book or any consequences thereof.

Author's Preface and Acknowledgements

This text has been written specifically to assist teachers and students to meet the requirements of CCEA's GCE History AS Unit 2, Option 5, 'Russia 1914–41'.

Divided into four parts to match the topics listed in the relevant section of CCEA's specification, this book will examine the complex and compelling story of the transformation of Russia (as it was in 1914) into the USSR (as it was in 1941). It will assist students when they are preparing for assessment tasks and help to validate independent research. The book will then look, in some detail, at the period's key figures and main concepts.

At the end of each chapter, there will be sample questions, to test students' knowledge and understanding. At the end of each section, there will also be specimen exam questions, complete with some guidance and examiner's advice on useful skills and techniques.

This book is for all my fellow historians and students who are interested in twentieth century Russian history. My thanks go out to the many historians and friends for their guidance and advice during the writing of this book. Special mention must be given to my good friend Richard Middleton, as without his support this book could not have been written. Finally, thanks to my editor Michelle Griffin for her consistent support and effort in bringing this book to fruition.

Jim McBride
May 2018

THE REVOLUTIONS OF FEBRUARY AND OCTOBER 1917

This chapter will examine:

1.1: The short-term factors that led to the downfall of tsarism in 1917.

1.2: The impact of the First World War on Russia by February 1917 and the economic, political and military consequences.

1.3: The political errors Tsar Nicholas II made in the run up to 1917 – including leaving the government in the hands of Tsarina Alexandra – and Rasputin's increasing influence.

1.4: The weaknesses and failures of the Provisional Government, the role of the soviets and Dual Authority.

1.5: The factors that led to the downfall of the Provisional Government such as its political mistakes which led to the Bolshevik seizure of power in October 1917.

1.6: The strengths of the Bolsheviks as well as the roles of their leaders, Lenin and Trotsky, in the October Revolution.

At the end of this chapter there will be a summary of the causes and effects of some of the key events in this period, along with some exam-style questions.

1.1: The Downfall of Tsar Nicholas II

On 1 August 1914 – five weeks after the assassination in Sarajevo, of Franz Ferdinand, Archduke of Austria – Germany declared war on Russia and the First World War truly began.

Despite some personal doubts about the wisdom of challenging the military might of the Central Powers, Tsar Nicholas II fully committed to the war effort once hostilities began. The Fourth Duma (the Russian assembly), with the exception of a few Bolshevik deputies, also pledged its unwavering support.

Very few Russian people foresaw the kind of trouble the war was going to cause, especially since the Central Powers, especially Germany, had feared what was known as 'the Russian steamroller'. At the time, Russia was a large, imperial power with territory that stretched across a dozen time zones, from the Baltic Sea in Europe to the Pacific Ocean in Asia. Within this territory were many different types of climate, many different cultures (for instance, almost one hundred different languages were spoken), and the population was growing rapidly – by 1914, the population of the Russian Empire more than 170 million.[1] Russia was like a heavy piece of machinery and, while the German government (and many other people) thought it would take a long time to mobilise Russia's huge army, they feared that, once it was in the field, its size would make it unstoppable. Everything in its path would be flattened.

But the war shone a blazing and unflattering spotlight on Nicholas II's reign, highlighting his refusal to allow further constitutional reform, and quickly laid bare problems that had been neglected for years. For many Russians at the beginning of the twentieth century, living conditions were archaic. More than 80 per cent of Russian citizens were peasants and many of them lived, as their ancestors had done for generations, in conditions reminiscent of the Middle Ages.

Society was dominated by the Imperial family, the aristocracy, the church, the civil service and the army, and the war exposed the frailties and failings of tsarist autocracy. It highlighted Nicholas II's character defects and his intransigence when faced with calls for political reform. For decades, long-term problems had been ignored, and vested interests within the ruling classes appeased, and when the war placed an enormous strain on both Russian society and the military, the tsar and his government were blamed.

Historians interpret the wartime period in Russia (and its consequences) in different ways. Some claim that, even in 1914, the end of the out-dated tsarist system was inevitable. Others argue that the country had been helped greatly by economic recovery after 1906 and by limited constitutional reform, and that Russia and its system of government were stable at the outbreak of war. It certainly seems that opposition to the regime was fragmented at that time. Political extremists had very little support and many of the leaders of such groups had been out of the country for years (in exile after a failed revolution in 1905).[2] This was one reason why the tsarist government was not very concerned.

The ineffectual and obstinate Tsar Nicholas II remained complacent and his lack of effective actions, combined with the short-term effects of war, led to his downfall in 1917.

Russia and its allies in the First World War, 1914.

CONSOLIDATE YOUR KNOWLEDGE

"The processions in the streets, carrying the tsar's portrait, framed by the flags of Russia's allies. The bands everywhere, playing the national anthem. Those first days of war! How full were we of enthusiasm; of the conviction that we were fighting, in just cause, for the freedom of the world! Swept away by the general air of excitement, we dreamt dreams of triumph; of victory. The war would be over by Christmas and the Cossacks would ride into Berlin."

Muriel Buchanan, daughter of the British Ambassador to Russia,
writing about the events of August 1914.

1. According to Buchanan (above), why did people in Russia welcome the outbreak of the First World War in August 1914?
2. How reliable is Buchanan as a source for historians wanting to know how popular the tsar's decision to go to war was?
3. Explain why Germany feared the entry of Russia into the war.

GROUP ACTIVITY

Organise a class debate with the motion:

"The collapse of tsarism was inevitable."

1.2: The Economic, Political and Military Effects of the First World War, 1914–17

The road to war and revolution, 1914–17
Key dates and events

1914	28 June 1914	Franz Ferdinand, Archduke of Austria, assassinated in Sarajevo.
	1 August 1914	Germany declares war on Russia.
	5 August 1914	Austria-Hungary declares war on Russia.
	August/September	Fourth Duma is suspended.
	August 1914	Russian defeat at Tannenberg. The capital St Petersburg is renamed Petrograd.
	September 1914	Russian defeat at the Masurian Lakes.
1915	Spring	German forces advance deep into Russian territory.
	June	The Progressive Bloc is formed.
	August	Nicholas II appoints himself commander-in-chief of the armed forces. Tsarina is left in charge of the government in Petrograd.
1916	Summer	The Brusilov Offensive is launched against Austria-Hungary.
	December	Rasputin murdered by a group of Russian aristocrats.
1917	February	Russian army on the verge of collapse. Strikes are widespread, especially in Petrograd.
	18 February–4 March	February Revolution and abdication of Tsar Nicholas II. Formation of Provisional Government.

Economic consequences

The Russian economy had started to recover after the Russo-Japanese War of 1904–05, and in 1914, several sectors were still experiencing growth.[3] Industrial production increased to meet the demands of the First World War, and wages rose.

Yet, while industrialisation boomed, workers endured terrible hardship and poverty, and lived in very poor conditions. Even in 1914, the country was less urbanised than the other major European powers and by 1915, the war was putting the economy under further strain. Discontent among Russian peasants and industrial workers began to grow.

After the harsh winter of 1916–17, the economy was on the verge of total collapse. Agricultural workers were badly affected by the war. Millions of them had been drafted into the army, their machines and animals requisitioned for the war effort, while many more moved to the cities, attracted by the prospect of work in the factories. The large influx of people from rural areas caused the urban proletariat (working classes) in Moscow and Petrograd combined, to swell in number from 22 million in 1914 to 28 million in 1916. By 1915–16 there were extensive labour shortages on farms and agricultural production fell.

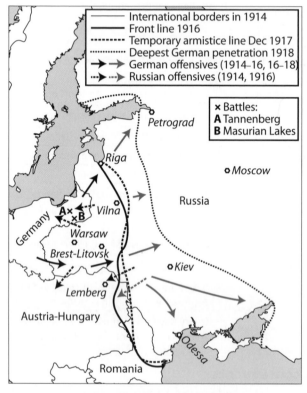

Russia and the Eastern Front, 1914–18.

By late 1916, almost 15 million men had been conscripted into the armed forces, and industrial production had also slumped as a result. Urban areas experienced severe food shortages, a problem that was compounded since the armed forces were given priority access to food over civilians. Soon, even bread had become scarce. Moscow, for example, needed 120 freight wagons of produce every day, but was receiving only 20 on average. The vast Russian railway network had struggled to cope with the demands war had made on the country and some railway lines had been blocked by unusable wagons, carriages or locomotives, or even by whole trains that had broken down. Food supplies, limited as they were, could take weeks rather than days to travel from the countryside to the cities. Most of the trains were being used to carry soldiers and military equipment rather than food, but the weather conditions (which were terrible, even by Russian standards) made rail transport between the Eastern Front, the main cities and rural areas almost impossible. The results were devastating.

The prices of food, fuel and everyday goods were driven up by inflationary pressure (in some cities inflation had reached 400 per cent), and millions of ordinary Russians, many of whom had already been living in poverty, now faced greater hardships. Labour strikes became commonplace as wage increases failed to keep up with the rate of inflation, which by late 1916, was almost out of control. Three main factors lay behind this. Firstly, there was the collapse of the railway network. Secondly, the military requirements of the army were a massive drain on resources and those demands were placed before the needs of civilians. Finally, there was the problem of the peasantry.

As prices for agricultural produce started to rise during 1915, peasants benefited. They could afford to hoard grain. As the rate of inflation rose throughout 1916, they stockpiled even more supplies, helping to create an upward spiral in the inflation rate. However, peasants weren't actually able to buy much, if anything since neither farm implements nor consumer goods were being produced. Therefore, peasants had no real incentive to sell their produce.

In September 1916, the chief of police in Petrograd had issued warnings about the threat that plummeting living standards posed to the survival of the government. Those affected by hardship included factory workers, office workers and government bureaucrats, and even some policemen. Yet the tsarist government ignored warnings such as this and failed to intervene in the growing economic crisis, resulting in unrest among ordinary people and helping to convert the masses into revolutionaries.

CONSOLIDATE YOUR KNOWLEDGE

1. How had the war effort affected industry by 1917?
2. What were the effects of the war effort on agriculture by 1917?
3. Explain how conditions for workers had worsened by 1917.
4. Why were railways so important to the war effort between 1914 and 1917?

Political consequences

After the outbreak of the war a wave of national patriotism surged across Russia. Most ordinary people were strongly in favour, and even the industrial strikes in Petrograd ceased for a while.

It wasn't just the masses who pledged their support. In August 1914, almost every political party in the Fourth Duma fully endorsed Russia's participation in the war. The only opposition came from the Bolshevik Party [see p.36], who were small, isolated and criticised for their views (they were even accused, at one point, of being German agents).[4]

Yet by 1916–17, this unity had been shattered by the ineffectiveness of the tsarist system of government. Incompetent execution of the war effort led to many political parties demanding immediate and wide-ranging reforms.

Most political leaders had expected that the war would be short and the outcome would be a successful one for Russia. Initial successes on the battlefield, however, were followed by punishing defeats at the hands of the German army. By the start of 1915, it was clear that the war was not going well for Russia on any part of the Eastern Front. By the middle of that year, losses were heavy and the government was being criticised for its failure to supply the army with the materiel (munitions in particular) that it required. As historian Richard Pipes commented:

> By June 1915, the spirit of common purpose that had united the government and opposition had vanished. This led to recriminations and hostility even more intense than the revolutionary mood of 1904–1905.[5]

In this period, one of the few consistent factors was the persistent refusal of the tsar to listen to political advice, whether it came from the Duma, his ministers or the representatives of friendly foreign governments. Grand Duke Michael, the tsar's popular younger brother, had already warned him that the tsarist system could collapse completely unless Nicholas introduced further political reforms.

In response to the tsar's inaction, 236 (out of a total number of 422) deputies in the Duma formed what became known as the 'Progressive Bloc' with members drawn from most of the parties. The main purpose of the Bloc was actually to preserve the existing system of government by helping win the war and by maintaining public support for the tsar. In August 1915, it drew up a legislative programme as part of plans to create a national government, the Ministry of National Confidence. The tsar dismissed their offer of support without hesitation, not realising that he had probably thrown away his last chance to reform and maintain the tsarist regime.

On 3 September 1915, Nicholas made what some historians regard as his final politically fatal error. It was an action that left him isolated from potential political allies. He prorogued (suspended) the Fourth Duma. This suspension was followed by a series of ministerial reshuffles, none of which was effective. In 1915–16, there were four prime ministers, three foreign ministers, six interior ministers and three war ministers. Each one is considered to have been a failure and so this policy of 'ministerial leapfrog', as it was dubbed at the time, helped to discredit the tsarist regime and bring about its downfall in 1917.[6]

The political crisis was somewhat eased in the first half of 1916 because the war seemed to be going better for Russia. In the second half of the year, however, the crisis returned and intensified, and by February 1917 there was no room for the kind of political compromises necessary for the tsarist system to survive.

Striking workers protesting outside the Duma in Petrograd, early 1917.
The slogans on the posters are demands for bread and land.

CONSOLIDATE YOUR KNOWLEDGE

5. Why, in 1914, did most political parties in Russia support the war?
6. Why were the Bolsheviks so politically unpopular in August 1914?
7. What was the Progressive Bloc and what were its political aims?
8. What political mistakes had the tsar made by February 1917?

Military consequences

The tsar's loyal soldiers welcomed the decision to go to war in August 1914. The so-called 'Russian Steamroller' made its way, with surprising speed, into the German province of East Prussia, before suffering massive defeats, towards the end of 1914, at Tannenberg and the Masurian Lakes. Some early successes against Austria-Hungary in Galicia had been reversed by the early part of 1915, when a military stalemate developed.

By the end of 1914, more than six million Russian soldiers had been mobilised, and the army, initially comprised of enthusiastic, loyal and experienced men, was now mostly made up of conscripts, many of whom were uneducated peasants. It was also vastly under-resourced – there were severe munitions shortages and some soldiers were sent to fight with no weapons or even a proper uniform. After just one year of war, roughly four million Russian soldiers had been killed, wounded, captured or were missing in action.

The tsar and his government were blamed for the failure of Russian industry to supply the army with the materiel it so desperately needed. Nicholas II intervened personally and in August 1915, with the aim of improving the conduct of the war, he made himself commander-in-chief of the armed forces. Despite his lack of combat experience and lack of ability, Nicholas believed that only he could command the army and lead it to victory. But far from being the decisive action the tsar thought it would be, this damaged his political authority and exposed his personal weaknesses in three key ways:

1. From that time he was blamed personally for the army's defeats and shortcomings.
2. The appointment revealed that he had neither the skills nor the temperament for such a demanding leadership role.

3. Now operating from general headquarters at Mogilev (737 km south of the capital), he became increasingly isolated from the home front and from the business of government and was therefore unable to react quickly when problems for civilians (particularly in cities) started to mount.

In the months immediately after Nicholas's assumption of the post, his decision did appear to have been vindicated. Russia staged something of a military comeback, as the army seemed to recover its strength: it had more troops and equipment than at any time since 1914. In fact, during the remainder of the First World War, it never again had as many troops or as much equipment. But this revival of fortunes lasted only until the summer of 1916.

Tsar Nicholas II visits Russian troops, 1915.

By June 1916, Russia was strong enough to launch a major offensive against Austro-Hungarian forces. Under the 'Brusilov Offensive' – named after Aleksei Brusilov, the general in charge of the operation – Russian forces advanced along a 480 km-long front, and took more than 200,000 Austro-Hungarian prisoners. However, about three months after the beginning of the offensive, the German army came to the aid of its Austro-Hungarian allies and the Russian advance was brought to a halt.

Brusilov was seen as a military hero at the time but the offensive had significantly depleted troop reserves – Russian forces suffered about 500,000 casualties with no real gains – and thus weakened the army's ability to fight further battles. Subsequently, they were not in a strong position to challenge German reinforcements in late 1916.

The nature of the Russian army changed utterly during the First World War as many of the able officers and loyal soldiers who had been in the tsar's service in 1914 had been lost in battle, replaced by conscripts who were little more than "peasants in uniform".[7] The harsh winter and materiel shortages in late 1916 to early 1917, severely affected the efficiency and discipline of ordinary soldiers. Unrest grew, and the number of desertions increased. Dreadful conditions and heavy losses destroyed military and public morale.

After taking personal control of the armed forces, the tsar may have appeared to deal with the problems affecting the army, but this was actually a political illusion. His persistent refusal to heed advice, along with the chaotic nature of his government and the associated political scandals, helped contribute to his downfall in February 1917. By that time, as economic unrest spread across Petrograd from the factories, and as the political problems accelerated out of control, even many senior generals – some of whom had been the pillars of tsarism – had enough of their weak yet stubborn ruler, believing that only a *coup d'état* could save Russia from another revolution.

The short-term effects of the First World War

Economic	Political	Military
• Inflation • Shortages of food and limited supplies • Limited industrialisation • Transport problems • Discontented peasants and industrial workers • Poor living conditions	• Entry into the war in 1914 led to political divisions in the Duma • Weak government with frequent ministerial changes • Growing demands for political reforms • The creation of the Progressive Bloc • The opposition of the tsar to any more political reforms • Loss of support from army and political elites	• The army suffered heavy defeats in 1914 • Loss of morale • Conscription of millions of resentful peasants • Shortages of weapons and materiel • Heavy losses of soldiers and equipment • Failure of Russian offensives • Generals' loss of faith in the tsar

CONSOLIDATE YOUR KNOWLEDGE

9. Why was the government's management of the war so ineffective during this period?

10. How did heavy Russian losses affect (a) the army, and (b) the people?

11. To what extent could Russia's military problems be blamed solely on Tsar Nicholas II?

GROUP ACTIVITY

Using the table on the short-term effects of the First World War, discuss the problems facing Russia by early 1917. Which of the three main factors was the most important in the downfall of tsarism in February 1917 and why?

1.3: The Misjudgements and Mistakes of Tsar Nicholas II

The influence of Tsarina Alexandra and Rasputin

In August 1914, the tsar helped to lead Russia into the First World War. This decision was warmly welcomed by his government, by the army and by the majority of the Russian people. However, it proved to be the first in a series of misjudgements that ultimately led to the February Revolution of 1917, destroying the autocratic system over which he had presided since 1894.

For the first twelve months of the war, Nicholas remained as the head of government in Petrograd (the capital had been renamed in September 1914 because it was felt that St Petersburg sounded too German), but, as already mentioned, the tsar appointed himself commander-in-chief of the armed forces in August 1915, when it appeared that the government was incapable of prosecuting the war effectively.

He appointed his German-born wife, Tsarina Alexandra, as regent in 1915 – she would have the responsibility of overseeing the government and would take responsibility for domestic policy. But even the most loyal supporters of tsarism couldn't really accept that the unpopular empress was the right person to rule Russia or defend the autocracy, especially with self-styled holy man, Gregori Rasputin, serving as her closest adviser. Rasputin had been a favourite of the tsarina, even before 1914 (her son, Alexei, suffered from haemophilia and Rasputin had been treating the boy since 1906), but he was extremely unpopular among courtiers – tales of his affairs with the wives of aristocrats and of his scandalous practices had been circulating for years.

In the months that followed her appointment as regent, the tsarina did nothing to improve her popularity. She dismissed and appointed ministers and their deputies in rapid succession – thirty-six different cabinet ministers held office at this time – and these were neither hired on the basis of ability nor fired for an absence of it, they were appointed according to the personal whims of the tsarina and Rasputin. Important supporters of Nicholas and of the autocratic system, (such as Mikhail Rodzianko, the presiding officer of the Duma; and General Mikhail Alekseyev, chief of the general staff) were alienated from the government, frustrated that able ministers were being removed from political office for no good reason. Many other courtiers, politicians and even ordinary Russians, were outraged, and some began referring to the tsarina as "that German woman".

Rumours then began to circulate that the empress and Rasputin (now exerting incredible influence at the imperial court) were having an affair and, while it is highly unlikely that this was true, it did increase the level of resentment towards the pair.

On 1 November 1916, during a speech in the State Duma, Pavel Milyukov – the leader of the Constitutional Democrats ('Kadets') – listed the government's repeated failures, punctuating each point with the question, "Is this stupidity or is it treason?"[8] The speech was highly inflammatory and a significant point on the road to the February Revolution, yet Nicholas once more refused to listen or to act.

The growing anger within the political elites came to a head in December 1916, with a conspiracy to murder Rasputin.[9] His death, however, did little to allay the people's concerns about how Russia was being governed, and by the end of 1916 political discontent continued to grow.[10] The tsarina had alienated aristocrats and members of other power elites (notably those high-ranking army officers who had been loyal to the regime even during the unsuccessful 1905 Revolution), and the political mistakes she and Rasputin made were contributory factors behind the February Revolution of 1917.

The February Revolution, 18 February–5 March 1917 [11]

On 18 February 1917, after issuing demands for higher wages because of the rising prices of food and goods, over 20,000 workers were locked out of the Putilov Steelworks by the authorities at the mill. This was the largest and most politically active factory in Petrograd and by 22 February, 100,000 people were demonstrating outside the plant. The situation deteriorated further on 23 February, when many more people came to the streets to mark International Women's Day and, within two days, Petrograd had been paralysed by a general strike. The sympathies of many police officers and even some soldiers lay with the protesters rather than the government.

The tsar and the system he had headed were now despised. People felt that the war and the economy had been totally mismanaged. Protests, strikes and demonstrations – against all aspects of tsarism – exploded across Petrograd.

The tsar sent a telegram ordering General Sergei Khabalov, the commander of the 180,000 troops in Petrograd, to disperse demonstrators, using live rounds if necessary. The tsar's situation had become hopeless. Army desertion was becoming commonplace, while units were beginning to disobey instructions from senior officers. When the Duma suggested that the tsar make concessions in order to preserve the monarchy, he responded by dissolving the parliament.

Having been influenced by his wife's wildly unrealistic assessment of the political and security situation in Petrograd, the tsar initially ignored a telegram from Rodzianko (president of the Duma) who was pleading for immediate action. However, on 28 February he decided to return to Petrograd, with the intention of regaining control of the city.

The royal train was stopped by soldiers at a small town on the Petrograd–Moscow railway line, approximately 160 km south east of Petrograd. The tsar was not allowed to proceed to the city itself and went instead to Pskov, about 200 km from the capital.

On 2 March, General Nikolai Ruzski arrived to see Nicholas, bringing with him a transcript of a telegraphic conversation he had had with Rodzianko. In Rodzianko's opinion, Nicholas had to abdicate. Ruzski passed the transcript to General Alekseyev (chief of the general staff), who re-transmitted it to commanding generals and asked for their comments. Most of them agreed that, to prevent mutiny and save the country from anarchy, the tsar would have to go. The 'Stavka' (general headquarters of the army) sent Nicholas a draft agreement or 'manifesto'. After a few minor alterations the tsar signed it and agreed to abdicate. By then, the tsarist system had become so discredited that no group was terribly interested in saving it.

Most historians will argue that the tsar was largely the author of his own misfortune, ignoring warnings time and again. By February 1917 he had brought tsarism to the brink of disaster in three main ways:

1. By February, almost 500,000 workers were on strike in Petrograd.
2. The effects of the war (and, in particular, the 8 million or more casualties) destroyed the natural allegiance of the Russian people to the tsar.
3. Nicholas' sheer incompetence caused him to lose the respect of former pillars of tsarism – the most important of these were his generals.

In the end, three hundred years of Romanov history had counted for very little. As Russian poet, Vladimir Mayakovsky, commented at the time, "Like the chewed stump of a fag, we spat their dynasty out".[12]

CONSOLIDATE YOUR KNOWLEDGE

1. What political mistakes did Nicholas make in 1915? What were the effects of those mistakes?
2. Why was the tsarina so unpopular in Russia after 1914?
3. What was the role of Rasputin between 1914 and 1916?
4. Why had the tsar lost the support of the powerful elites by 1917?
5. What were the immediate causes of the February Revolution?

GROUP ACTIVITY

Organise a class debate with the motion:

"The actions of Nicholas II were solely to blame for his downfall in February 1917."

1.4: The Provisional Government, the Petrograd Soviet and the Problem of Dual Authority

Russia moves towards liberal democracy
Key dates and events

1 March 1917	Petrograd Soviet issues 'Order No 1', its first major statement.
2 March 1917	Abdication of the tsar. Formation of Provisional Government.
3 April 1917	Lenin returns to Petrograd by train. Speech to followers at the Finland Station, Petrograd, outlining his 'April Theses', written during the journey.
3–6 July 1917	'The July Days' (failed Bolshevik *coup d'état*).
8 July 1917	Kerensky succeeds Prince Lvov as chairman of the Provisional Government (in effect, prime minister).
25–30 August 1917	Kornilov affair
1 September 1917	Formal proclamation of republic by Provisional Government.
25 September 1917	Bolsheviks take control of Petrograd Soviet, with Leon Trotsky as chairman.
9 October 1917	Trotsky sets up Military Revolutionary Committee (MRC).
25–26 October 1917	Bolsheviks seize power during October Revolution.

The Provisional Government

The February Revolution had been spontaneous and unplanned. It happened so quickly that many people, both inside and outside Russia, were taken by surprise.

When the tsar was forced to abdicate, a caretaker government soon emerged. Twelve members of the Duma had decided to ignore the tsar's prorogation order and instead formed the 'Provisional Committee of the State Duma for Restoring Law and Order' that then became known as the 'Provisional Government'. Its two most urgent objectives were taking control of the country and making the transition to liberal democracy.

Opposition groups denounced the Provisional Government as being unrepresentative and questioned its legitimacy, but the new temporary administration promised that an election would be held for a Constituent Assembly that would draw up a new, democratic constitution. The first chairman of the Provisional Government was Prince Georgy Lvov. To gain public support, the Provisional Government needed to appear decisive and to introduce measures that would keep the masses satisfied, but, for the most part, it failed on both counts.

Far from appearing united and decisive, the Provisional Government was a coalition of different political parties. At first it was dominated by the moderate Socialist Revolutionary Party (SRs) and the Kadets, but soon, even smaller parties like the Mensheviks would be represented, and this made it difficult to make important political decisions.

Certainly, the government did introduce a number of progressive measures in its early days: trade unions were legalised; factory workers were promised an eight-hour day; civil and religious liberties were guaranteed; the old Imperial Police were replaced with a people's militia; the tsarist secret police (the Okhrana) were disbanded; and an amnesty for political prisoners was declared, allowing exiled opponents of tsarism and extremists – such as Vladimir Ilyich Ulyanov (Lenin) [see p.36] – to return to Russia.[13] However, the working-class and lower-middle-class remained sceptical about the new administration's ability to fulfil its promises.

CONSOLIDATE YOUR KNOWLEDGE

1. Which main parties made up the Provisional Government in March 1917?
2. What were their political aims when they took power?
3. What problems did the Provisional Government face in March 1917?

The soviets

The Provisional Government's coalition status may have led to internal power struggles, but that was not the only issue it faced. From the beginning its ability to act decisively was greatly reduced by the presence of the soviets in Russia.

The soviets were a kind of local council or assembly, established and elected by Russian workers, and had first sprung up during the short-lived 1905 Revolution. They were mostly comprised of trade unionists, although other interests (such as cooperative societies and left-wing political parties) were often represented too. In fact, until the summer of 1917, soviets were generally dominated by more moderate socialists, such as the Socialist Revolutionaries or the Mensheviks.

The Petrograd Soviet was by far the most powerful.[14] It had emerged in February 1917, had more than 3,000 delegates and its executive committee wielded considerable influence. It, rather than the Provisional Government, had effective control over some public services in the capital, over the people's militia (which had taken the place of the old Imperial Police) and over the city's military garrison.

Dual Authority

On 1 March 1917, the Petrograd Soviet issued 'Soviet Order Number 1', a document that, for the most part, was concerned with new rules for military personnel. However, the fourth point in the Order was crucial in weakening the authority of the Provisional Government. It gave the soviet's orders supremacy over those of the new government, if there was any conflict of interest between the two bodies.

> All orders issued by the Military Commission of the State Duma [i.e. the Provisional Government] shall be carried out, except those which run counter to the orders and decrees issued by the Soviet of Workers' and Soldiers' Deputies.[16]

In practice, the strange division of governmental responsibilities now meant that the Provisional Government did not have complete control over the Russian army, yet this 'Dual Authority' was surprisingly effective for a while. Throughout March and April, in the immediate aftermath of the February Revolution, the Petrograd Soviet and the Provisional Government worked well together. The Petrograd Soviet had not originally intended to become a rival to government, and many political figures – such as Alexander Kerensky (leader of the Socialist Revolutionary Party and prime minister from August 1917 [see p.207]) – were members of both bodies. Since the soviets – which in these early days were mainly dominated by the Mensheviks, and not the Bolsheviks in Moscow and Petrograd – represented workers and soldiers, while ordinary people used them more as a forum in which to air their grievances.

However, as the disastrous war continued through the summer of 1917, soviets came under greater Bolshevik influence and control. The increase in the soviets' power made plain the flaws in the Dual Authority system and the political significance of Order Number 1. It was soon clear that, by agreeing to share power with the soviets after the end of tsarism, the Provisional Government had made a significant political error.

CONSOLIDATE YOUR KNOWLEDGE

4. What was the relationship between the Provisional Government and the Fourth Duma?
5. What economic problems did the Provisional Government face when it assumed power?
6. What was Dual Authority?
7. Explain the political importance of Order Number 1 of the Petrograd Soviet.
8. Why did the Petrograd Soviet have so much political influence?

The failings of the Provisional Government

If agreeing to Dual Authority had been the Provisional Government's first error, its second mistake was to promise political reforms that it was unable to deliver. It also decided to wait until the Constituent Assembly was elected before implementing any major reforms (such as land reforms). Its third serious error was the tremendously unpopular decision to keep Russia in the First World War. The effects of these errors were disastrous and would be ruthlessly exploited by the Bolsheviks in the summer of 1917.

Ultimately, the decision to go on fighting Germany after the tsar's abdication may have damaged the new government, but the reasons behind it are not hard to understand. Russia was heavily dependent on supplies and financial aid from her Western allies. Had Russia withdrawn from the war in 1917, it would have risked bankruptcy, and a German occupation might well follow the resultant financial catastrophe. The new government thought that staying in the war would be the least worst option.

It was also felt that, if Russian forces could hold out for a few more months and the Allies could win (perhaps with American help, as indeed they did by November 1918), then Russia might even make territorial gains from Germany at a peace conference. But if Russia were to make peace with Germany separately, before the whole conflict had come to an end, those potential gains would be lost.

It cannot be denied, however, that the war distracted the government from pressing social and economic difficulties at home: problems that had been magnified by the war. The new administration was confronted by three major internal issues:

1. Constituent assembly
2. Land reform
3. Economic crisis

There was also the question of national self-determination. Large ethnic groups within the Russian Empire – such as the Finns, Ukrainians and Georgians – desired independence, but the tsar had suppressed the nationalities issue. Now with the emergence of the new regime the issue was being raised again, so the Provisional Government asked representatives of the various nationalities to be patient while more urgent problems were addressed.

The government had given its word that elections to a Constituent Assembly would be held. This would have been the first representative and democratic body in modern Russian history and it was hoped that it would, among other things, legitimise the new regime and radically reform land ownership for the peasants. However, the practical difficulties of holding an election during the First World War, in such a large country, were obvious. Prime Minister Kerensky, also fearful of the demand that millions of new voters would place on the government, delayed elections to the Constituent Assembly, losing the support of many ordinary people.

The government also seemed to be backtracking on its promises of land reform. It had agreed that peasants should own the land on which they worked, and during the summer of 1917, many peasants began to desert from the army, believing that they would be able to claim ownership of their land. Frustrated by the wait for action, many peasants took the law into their own hands and seized property from the owners of country estates and very large farms. Ownership disputes and land seizures involving peasants led to falls in agricultural production.

People across Russia were losing faith in the Provisional Government. Like its tsarist predecessor, it was beset by economic problems and its conduct of the war was unsatisfactory. The economic problems may have been inherited from Nicholas II but they had continued to worsen. Food and fuel shortages intensified as, due to the impact of the war and the ongoing land ownership disputes, agricultural production continued to suffer.

People queuing for food, Petrograd 1917. Factory workers were still experiencing food and fuel shortages, and other forms of hardship Their demands became more and more extreme during 1917.

CONSOLIDATE YOUR KNOWLEDGE

9. Why did the Provisional Government decide to keep Russia in the First World War?

10. What were the political consequences of this decision within Russia?

11. Describe the political demands that the Provisional Government faced in March 1917.

12. Why were elections for the Constituent Assembly delayed?

13. Why was the Provisional Government reluctant to deal with the issue of land reform?

1.5: Factors That Led to the Downfall of the Provisional Government

The Provisional Government was undoubtedly in a precarious situation, facing significant issues and under pressure from all sides. It is possible that, given some time, the new regime could have managed to stabilise the country, but three significant events came in quick succession, drastically weakening its position:

- The June Offensive
- The July Days
- The Kornilov Affair

The June Offensive

In June 1917, the Provisional Government made a last, frantic attempt to achieve a military breakthrough in the First World War. At that point, Alexander Kerensky was war minister, and, on his orders, the June Offensive was launched on the South-Western Front. After three weeks, it had not achieved any of its objectives. The Russian army had lost the will to fight – entire regiments mutinied and soldiers were deserting in large numbers. During the failed offensive, there were an estimated 60,000 Russian casualties, increasing unrest in Petrograd still further.

The July Days

By the start of July, problems on the home front were even worse than they had been in the spring: the people were dissatisfied with the government's conduct of the war (and with the unsuccessful June Offensive in particular); economic problems were still growing; soviets had spread across Russia; sailors, soldiers and labourers at Kronstadt (a naval base on an island near Petrograd) had set up a rival government; peasants were seizing land by force from their landlords; more and more factories were being taken over by workers; and the question of independence for the Ukraine provoked further protests in Petrograd.

From 3–7 July 1917 a series of spontaneous armed demonstrations occurred across Petrograd. The insurgents hoped to challenge the Provisional

Government and force the soviets to assume power. However, since they were generally unplanned, the risings were poorly organised. There was no effective leadership for the rebels, and their aims were unclear.

Once the Provisional Government had restored order in Petrograd, the Bolsheviks were blamed for the chaos – after all, most of the demonstrators were Bolshevik Party followers, and Lenin had openly declared, in June, that he and his supporters were ready to take power in Russia. Some Bolshevik leaders, such as Lev Kamenev and Leon Trotsky, were arrested. Others, such as Lenin who had been denounced as a German agent, avoided arrest by crossing into Finland.

The July Days appeared to have failed and served only to discredit the Bolsheviks, certainly, most ordinary people now seemed to hold the party in low regard, however, Lenin and Trotsky learned valuable lessons from the experience and put them to good use in October 1917.

Troops loyal to the Provisional Government firing on demonstrators during the July Days. Corner of Nevsky Prospect and Sadovaya Street, Petrograd, 1917.

The Kornilov Affair

General Lavr Kornilov had been the commander in charge of the June Offensive.[16] For some time, he had wanted to neutralise the revolutionary threat and, on 19 July, he was made commander-in-chief. Kornilov's plan was to send his most loyal troops to Petrograd, to restore law and order fully and deal with the Bolsheviks.

When Kerensky, now prime minister, learned of Kornilov's plan, he was perturbed. Was the general about to stage a *coup d'état*? Might he even restore the Romanov Dynasty? In a state of panic, Kerensky turned to the Bolsheviks in the hope that they would save the Provisional Government from, what he saw as, a reactionary menace. The Red Guards (an armed Bolshevik group) were mobilised while Bolshevik prisoners were released from prison and armed. The Petrograd Soviet also mobilised its forces. Kerensky's apparent betrayal of Kornilov caused the troops to desert the general and Kornilov was arrested.

Without Kerensky's interference, the Kornilov Affair might arguably have blown over. However, Kerensky had been so eager for his government to be saved that he had made his strongest opponents, the Bolsheviks, even stronger. And now they were well armed while the Russian army appeared to be in a state of disarray.

Soldiers at the front reading a Bolshevik newspaper, 13 July 1917.
Bolshevik publications were banned after the July Days.

The weaknesses and political mistakes of the Provisional Government

Weaknesses	Political Mistakes
• Dual Authority • Failing to hold elections to a Constituent Assembly • Failing to deliver land reforms • Lack of political legitimacy	• Keeping Russia in the First World War • The handling of the July Days • The handling of the Kornilov Affair • The role Kerensky played

TASK

Using the points above, and your own knowledge, what do you think was the most important factor in the downfall of the Provisional Government by October 1917?

CONSOLIDATE YOUR KNOWLEDGE

1. Why had Kerensky become an unpopular political leader by the summer of 1917?
2. Explain Kerensky's political errors and the effects of these mistakes by October 1917?
3. Why was Kerensky an important political figure during the events of 1917?
4. "The collapse of the June Offensive dealt a fatal blow to the authority of the Provisional Government. The fragile coalition fell apart, creating a power vacuum which led to the July uprisings."[17] To what extent do you agree with this verdict?

1.6: The Bolsheviks and Their Role in the October Revolution, 1917

Lenin

Born Vladimir Iliych Ulyanov, this son of a senior civil servant became a radical in his student days (perhaps in part because his brother, Sasha, had been executed in 1887 for trying to assassinate Tsar Alexander III, Nicholas II's father). Vladimir, better known by the pseudonym 'Lenin', became a lifelong Marxist (Communist) revolutionary. He was a member of the Russian Social Democratic Labour Party (RSDLP), and in 1903, when the party split into two factions, Bolshevik and Menshevik [see p.49], he became leader of the Bolsheviks.

Despite his best efforts the Bolsheviks were a tiny, fringe party who achieved very little electoral success or public recognition. Then, following the failed 1905 Revolution, Lenin became an isolated political figure, living outside Russia in exile (as indeed were many of the other Bolshevik leaders). As a result, he was not immediately aware of the evolving political scene in Russia between 1906 and 1914 and, as late as 1913, he had told supporters he doubted that there would be a successful Communist revolution in Russia within his lifetime. The First World War would change this outlook.

The Bolsheviks had been the only Russian political party to oppose the war in 1914, and at its outbreak they, along with socialists across Europe, expected workers to rise against their oppressive governing classes and frustrate what was seen as an imperialist enterprise. "Turn the imperialist war into a civil war!" Lenin had urged.[18] He was living in neutral Switzerland at the time, and had continued to dream about violent Marxist revolution. While many other Bolsheviks had lost hope that there would ever be a successful Communist revolution, least of all in backward Russia, Lenin now felt that the country might be ripe for revolution, if the war went very badly.

Then in 1917, when an unprecedented sequence of events led to the February Revolution, it seemed that Lenin had, for the second time in his life, missed an opportunity to stir up a Communist revolution. He was living in Zurich at the time and feared that his career as a political agitator might be over.

The 'April Theses', April–July 1917

When news of the tsar's abdication reached Lenin and his exiled followers, they decided to return to Russia immediately to improve the Bolshevik chances of success. Lenin was also concerned that, in his absence, some Bolsheviks would compromise and cooperate with other socialist parties, perhaps even with the Provisional Government. In March 1917 he expressed the opinion that a second, socialist revolution would be needed, "Only a proletarian republic, backed by the rural workers and the poorest section of the peasants and town dwellers, can secure peace, provide bread, order and freedom."[19]

However, Lenin was in neutral Switzerland and, in order to reach Russia by a reasonably direct route, he would have to travel though Germany. In the end, it was the German government who came to Lenin's assistance. It hoped that Lenin would stir up revolutionary fervour, forcing Russia to withdraw from the war, and so it provided the famous sealed train.[20] This transported Lenin and his followers to the Baltic coast of Germany, from where he crossed to neutral Sweden, then Finland.

On 3 April 1917, he arrived at Finland Station, Petrograd and declared to the large crowd who had gathered there, "No support must be given to the Provisional Government."[21] He had, in effect, declared war on the new administration. As Prime Minister Kerensky remarked, "Just you wait, Lenin himself is coming, then the real thing will begin!"[22]

The next day, in spite of some doubts from other senior Bolsheviks, Lenin revealed his 'April Theses', a series of ten Bolshevik directives that he had prepared on his journey to Petrograd. In these, he attacked the "imperialist war", advocated the overthrow of the Provisional Government and supported the transfer of "All power to the Soviets".[23]

The Bolsheviks were able to use the 'April Theses' to great effect: Lenin's aims were significant and he had given the party clear political objectives. Through his popular slogan, "Peace, Bread and Land", he had identified the three main ways in which the Provisional Government had failed: it had not ended the war, resolved the food shortages or delivered reform in land ownership

Bolshevik propaganda skilfully exploited the Provisional Government's shortcomings and mistakes, leading to increased support for the party, yet by June 1917 it still had fewer than 200,000 members, and these were mainly in Petrograd and Moscow. Lenin knew that the party was too weak to stage a full Communist revolution, but he saw the soviets as a potential revolutionary vehicle and so he encouraged Bolsheviks to take control. Speaking in June 1917, he asserted that the Bolshevik Party was "ready to take over full power at any moment."[24]

Little by little, the Bolsheviks were consolidating their position, and if an opportunity soon emerged, the time would be right for their long-awaited proletariat revolution.

CONSOLIDATE YOUR KNOWLEDGE

1. Why did Lenin privately welcome the advent of the First World War in 1914?
2. Why did the Bolsheviks publicly oppose the war in 1914?
3. When the February Revolution started, why was Lenin's position so weak?
4. Why did Germany help Lenin to return to Russia?
5. What were Lenin's political demands in April 1917?
6. Explain the political impact of the 'April Theses'.
7. Explain the importance of Bolshevik propaganda in gaining popular support during 1917?

The Road to Power, July–October 1917

Since Lenin's return in April, support for the Bolsheviks had been growing – mainly among factory workers. Dissatisfaction with the army's disastrous June Offensive had led to the street protests of the 'July Days' [see p.32] and some Bolsheviks wanted to take charge of these, but Lenin had been in Finland for a period of convalescence and they had hesitated in his absence. When Lenin returned, he found that Prime Minister Kerensky had already restored law and order.

Kerensky was quick to blame the July Days on Lenin – whom he had dubbed "The German agent" – and the rest of the Bolsheviks, so he ordered their detention in an attempt to suppress the party. Lenin managed to avoid arrest by fleeing across the border and into Finland once again where, in July 1917, he wrote "Either complete victory for the military dictatorship or victory for the armed uprising of the workers."[25]

The Bolsheviks had been condemned in public, the party left in a state of disarray and Lenin's position appeared to be weaker than ever before. However, in a few short weeks came the Kornilov Affair [see p.33] and the Bolsheviks would secure the most unlikely of allies – Kerensky.

In order to defend the Provisional Government from the threat which (in Kerensky's eyes) General Kornilov had posed to it, Kerensky had turned, in desperation, to the Bolsheviks and the soviets: the Petrograd Soviet was mobilised; Bolshevik prisoners were released from prison; and The Red Guards were issued with government rifles.

When Kornilov was defeated, the Bolsheviks used their propaganda to portray themselves as the only group prepared to defend the revolution, and the rights of soldiers, workers and peasants. Many historians argue that, during the Kornilov Affair, Kerensky played right into Lenin's hands and generated momentum which led straight to the October Revolution.

The Bolsheviks' popularity rose during the summer partly because they were finally able to appeal to peasants. In April 1917, when Lenin had returned to Petrograd, he had said that the party wasn't ready to take part in a proletarian revolution. At that time, the Bolsheviks did not have a policy on the land issue, but by the middle of 1917, that had changed. Peasants were acting as a truly revolutionary force, seizing the land they worked from landowners.

Lenin was forced to change his tactics and to reach out to them, arguing that unique circumstances now prevailed in Russia. He adopted a new slogan, "Land to the peasants", and promised that the Bolsheviks would let peasants keep the land that they had already seized. This boosted Bolshevik support among peasants and helped spread anarchy across the Russian countryside. Lenin had actually stolen the land-reform policy of Kerensky's Socialist Revolutionary Party and adopted it as the Bolsheviks' own! This helped to split and weaken the SRs, and few of them, who agreed with Bolshevik policies, became known as the "Left SRs".

Leon Trotsky

It was during the summer of 1917 that the Bolsheviks would also find a great asset in the form of Leon Trotsky, a former Menshevik who had joined their party on 2 July 1917.

Thanks to his former Menshevik politics (and partly due to his Jewish background) many other senior members of the party did not trust him, but after the Kornilov Affair, Trotsky had emerged as a Bolshevik leader, second in importance only to Lenin.

By September, Bolsheviks had majorities within the soviets of both Petrograd and Moscow and, on 25 September, Trotsky was elected chairman of the Petrograd Soviet. On 12 October, he set up the Military Revolutionary Committee (MRC) with the ostensible aim of defending the capital city against another Kornilov-style attack, or against German forces. However, the MRC effectively became another armed wing of the Bolshevik Party.

By early October 1917, the Petrograd Soviet was shifting sharply to the left, while the Provisional Government was moving to the right. This made the continuation of Dual Authority [see p.28] impossible, and it became extremely difficult for anyone to govern Russia effectively.

CONSOLIDATE YOUR KNOWLEDGE

8. Why did the Bolshevik leadership actually play a very limited role in the July Days?
9. What were the consequences of the July Days for the Bolsheviks?
10. How did the Kornilov Affair assist the Bolshevik cause?
11. Explain how the Bolsheviks strengthened their position during September 1917.

The strengths of the Bolsheviks and the October Revolution

The Bolsheviks were growing rapidly as a political party and as a revolutionary movement, and most of their support was based in Moscow and Petrograd in particular. Their policies became more popular and support for the Provisional Government steadily declined. The Mensheviks and the SRs had been damaged by their collaboration with Kerensky's failing government. By September, many of their supporters were switching to the Bolsheviks. They were attracted by Lenin's simple, popular policies and by the apparent strength of his party.

In March 1917 the Bolsheviks had about 11,000 members. By October, they claimed to have more than 300,000 members. People in Russia were now shifting towards political extremes, creating a situation in which a second Socialist revolution would be possible.

Lenin returned to Russia on 7 October to address a secret meeting, on 10 October, of the central committee of the Social Democratic Labour Party (as the Bolsheviks' party was formally called). Some leading members, such as Kamenev, still opposed the seizure of power by force. Kamenev was worried that a coup could be crushed and that defeat would be utterly devastating to the Bolsheviks. Lenin, however, demanded that Bolshevik forces carry out a *coup d'état* immediately, "History will not forgive us, if we do not take power now."[26] He felt that the Bolsheviks had to act before the All-Russian Congress of Soviets met – this was the supreme governing body of the soviets, with representatives elected from all across Russia – and before elections to the Constituent Assembly were held.

In the end, and somewhat ironically, it was Kerensky who forced Lenin's hand. On 23 October, Kerensky tried to clamp down on Bolshevik activities by, for example, banning their newspapers, among which was *Pravda*. But the Bolsheviks were in a much stronger position than they had been only weeks earlier, and largely thanks to Trotsky, they held control of the Petrograd and Moscow soviets, and the MRC.

Trotsky had already drawn up plans for an armed revolutionary operation – which, in the first instance, would involve taking control of Petrograd's essential services, such as public transport, electricity generation, gas distribution and so on – and on 24 and 25 October 1917, following his model, the Provisional Government had been overthrown. The whole operation had taken only thirty-six hours.

Some of the government ministers and senior officials were captured by Bolshevik insurgents at the Winter Palace, but Kerensky donned a disguise and escaped in an ambulance. He made it to Pskov, and found troops prepared to retake Petrograd but their assault was unsuccessful. He remained hidden in Russia until May 1918, when he left for Western Europe. He lived in Paris and then, from 1940 onwards, in the New York area. He never returned to Russia but was an academic and anti-Bolshevik commentator on Russian affairs until a few years before his death in 1970.

In the end, the revolution had been a resounding success, with hardly a shot fired.[27] As Trotsky famously said to former members of the Provisional Government, "Your role is played out. Go where you belong ... into the dustbin of history".[28] The government hadn't been able to depend on the loyalty of soldiers and sailors in Petrograd, as many of these "peasants in uniform" (uneducated men from rural areas) had Bolshevik sympathies. In the same way, most urban factory workers, especially in the key cities of Moscow and Petrograd, had come to see the Bolsheviks as the only group that could take Russia out of the war and thereby ease their economic hardship

Lenin declared that the Bolsheviks had taken power on behalf of "all the soviets".[29] In addition, the Bolsheviks claimed to represent the soldiers of the garrison in Petrograd and sailors at the Kronstadt naval base. The latter had supported the abortive July Days. These factors help to explain the swift collapse of the discredited Provisional Government once Trotsky and the MRC had taken control of key public services. Even Stalin, writing in 1918, gave Trotsky more credit for the Bolsheviks' successful putsch than he gave Lenin.

Trotsky wrote about the events of 1917 in his book *A History of the Russian Revolution* (first published in 1930). He described the October Revolution as "a chain of objective historic forces" and that Lenin had been "a great link in that chain".[30] Without Lenin's decisive and single-minded leadership, it is unlikely that the October Revolution would have been so successful.

Historians debate the importance of Lenin and the success of the Bolsheviks in October 1917. John Laver describes the Bolshevik victory, as "an extraordinary event" and that the high-ranking Bolsheviks, Kamenev and Zinoviev, were correct when they labelled Lenin's plans a "gamble".[31] While Graham Darby ascribes the Bolsheviks' success to the many and varied flaws of the Provisional Government:

> From February onwards, the Provisional Government was simply drained of power as ordinary people took matters into their own hands … what little power the government had left, evaporated.[32]

Even Lenin, writing after the Bolshevik seizure of power, remarked that his assumption of power was as easy as "picking up a feather".[33]

CONSOLIDATE YOUR KNOWLEDGE

12. What were the aims of the Military Revolutionary Committee during the October Revolution?
13. Explain the importance of Trotsky's actions before the October Revolution.
14. Why did Lenin feel that the Bolsheviks had to put their plans into action in October 1917?

GROUP ACTIVITY

Discuss the various causes of the October Revolution. Using these, and your own research, prepare for a class debate on the most important reasons for the success of the October Revolution.

Revision Section: 1914–17

To improve knowledge and understanding, here is a quick overview of the key events between 1914 and October 1917, right up to "the ten days that shook the world"[35]. If used along with some sample exam papers, it will consolidate knowledge of these key events and help students prepare for their assessment unit tests. It is important to understand the impact of those key stages on the Russian state and people.

Independent research, looking at the key figures and events, will help students develop an understanding of the two revolutions that took place in 1917 and the way in which they contributed to Bolshevik success under Lenin's leadership

There is a list of useful books on this period on page 217.

Turning point 1: Russia in 1914

Students need to examine both the long-term and short-term problems that Russia was experiencing when it went to war in 1914. The effects of the First World War not only made some of those existing problems worse but also created new ones.

Long-term problems	Short-term-problems
• Role of tsar/government	• Growing political unrest
• Limited political reform	• Growing economic problems
• Conditions for peasants	• Restricted industrial development
• Condition for industrial workers	• Tsar's opposition to further reform
• Huge land area of Russia	• Reform of land ownership not complete
• Number of different ethnic groups, nationalities and languages	• Fourth Duma weak (and seen by masses as tool of businessmen and property owners)
• Problems with communication systems, transport etc.	• Political demands of bourgeoisie
• Revolutionary threat	

Turning point 2: The February Revolution

The events of February 1917 are very significant and it is essential to understand both its causes and effects.

Causes	Effects
• Role of tsar	• Downfall of tsarist system of government
• Roles of tsarina and Rasputin	
• Weak Russian government	• Provisional Government established
• Tsar blamed for ineffective prosecution of war	• Political reform promised
	• Constituent Assembly promised
• Military problems	• Land reforms promised
• Economic problems	• Dual Authority
• Inflation and shortages	• Rise of soviets
• Poor communications and transport problems	• Return of Bolsheviks
	• Economic problems unsolved
• Duma weak and then dismissed	• Russia stayed in war
• Alienation of elites	• Provisional Government lacked legitimacy and public support
• Growing political unrest	
• Heavy Russian casualties on battlefield	

Turning point 3: October 1917

This was the second and more important revolution of 1917. The October Revolution changed world history and it is essential to be aware of both its causes and the immediate effects. The roles played by the weak Provisional Government must be compared with the (ultimately successful) revolutionary leadership of Lenin and Trotsky.

Causes	Effects
• Continuing economic problems	• Provisional Government overthrown
• Effects of war effort	• Bolshevik seizure of power
• Shortages and hardship	• Lenin becomes head of Russian government
• Errors of Provisional Government	
• Role of Kerensky	• World's first Communist state
• Land issue unresolved	• Most Russians shocked
• Discontent of workers	• Western opposition

Causes ...	Effects ...
• Military problems	• Third form of government in one year
• Lenin's return	• Further political instability
• April Theses	
• Growth of Bolsheviks	
• July Days	
• Kornilov Affair	
• Role of Trotsky and the MRC	
• Role of Petrograd Soviet	

PRACTICE EXAMINATION QUESTIONS, 1914–17

Based on format of questions for CCEA Unit AS2, Option 5 (Russia)

These questions are for individual or class-based use and study. Questions from past papers and specimen papers can be accessed through the CCEA GCE History microsite.

www.rewardinglearning.org.uk/microsites/history/gce/past_papers/index.asp

These are some sample 8-mark and 22-mark examination-type questions, which will help students to prepare and practice for assessment tasks for this period.

8-mark questions (short responses)

a) Explain the political problems that Russia faced in 1914.

b) Explain Russia's economic problems in 1914.

c) Explain the military effects of the First World War.

d) Explain the short-term causes of the February Revolution.

e) Explain the political mistakes made by the Provisional Government in 1917.

f) Explain the short-term causes of the October Revolution.

22-mark questions (essay answers)

- To what extent did the political mistakes made by Nicholas II personally contribute to his downfall in February 1917?
- "The economic effects of the First World War were the most important cause of the February Revolution." To what extent do you accept this verdict?
- "Without Lenin's political leadership, the Bolsheviks would not have been successful in October 1917." How accurate do you think this assessment is?
- To what extent were the Provisional Government's own mistakes responsible for bringing about its collapse in October 1917?

Endnotes

1   Despite its size and power, however, at that time Russia still used the Julian 'old style' (OS) calendar. Most other European countries had long since switched to the Gregorian 'new style' (NS) calendar, meaning Russia was literally 13 days behind the rest of the world, and would remain so until the calendars changed in February 1918. The 'old style' dates will be used throughout this chapter until the 'new style' dates become applicable.

2   On 9 January 1905, the army opened on a peaceful demonstration outside the Winter Palace in St Petersburg. Hundreds were killed, leading to a series of strikes and riots. By October 1905 a general strike had spread across Russia and workers and sailors had set up committees (soviets) to represent them.

3   Though it should be noted that a number of western-European countries, such as France, had poured money into Russia's pre-war industrial expansion and, by 1914, Russia was Europe's largest debtor nation.

4   The Mensheviks and Bolsheviks were originally part of the same political party, the Social Democratic Labour Party (RSDLP, SDs or Social Democrats), before it split into two factions in 1903. The Mensheviks (minority), led by Julius Martov accepted that Russia was not ready for a Marxist revolution but felt that it was bound to happen in the long term. The Bolsheviks (majority), led by Lenin, believed that a dedicated revolutionary elite could seize power and then set about creating a socialist state in Russia, provided that its revolution was well planned.

5   Pipes, Richard, *The Russian Revolution*, eBook (Knopf, 1990)

6   The term was coined by right-wing politician Vladimir Purishkevich on 19 November 1916; *see* Figes, Orlando, *A People's Tragedy: A History of the Russian Revolution* (Jonathan Cape, 1996), p.278

7   Bushnell, John, 'Peasants in Uniform: The Tsarist Army as a Peasant Society', *Journal of Social History*, Vol. 13, Issue 4, (July 1980)

8   Milyukov, Pavel, 'Rasputin and Rasputuiza', 1 November 1916, State Duma

9   Rasputin was invited to a party and poisoned with cyanide powder hidden in cream cakes and wine. When this seemed to have little apparent effect, the plotters (which included four well-connected socialites and an army officer) shot the self-styled healer but, to the horror of those present, he managed to make his way outside, blood pouring from his mouth. He was shot several times in the back, before he finally died. His body was later dumped into the River Neva.

10 Most historians paint Rasputin in a negative light but he did make a few sound political decisions and displayed some administrative skill: reorganising the army's medical supply chain, for instance.

11 These are the Julian (OS) calendar dates. The citizens of Petrograd would give the date of the February Revolution as 22 February 1917, though this would have been 7 March 1917 for the rest of the world.

12 Perry, K., *Modern European History*, eBook (Made Simple, 1991)

13 The first group of Bolshevik prisoners released by the Provisional Government arrived in Petrograd in the middle of March 1917. Notably, leading figures in the Bolshevik

Party – such as Stalin, Molotov and Kamenev – did not denounce the Provisional Government when they arrived in Petrograd.

14 Known in full as The Petrograd Soviet of Workers' and Soldiers' Deputies.

15 Karl Marx (1818–83) was a German revolutionary and philosopher.

16 The Petrograd Soviet of Workers' and Soldiers' Deputies, 'Soviet Order Number 1', 1 March 1917 (OS)

17 To prevent mass desertion from the army at that time, Kornilov had demanded that the government reinstate the death penalty for courts-martial. Kerensky had agreed.

18 Figes, Orlando, *Revolutionary Russia, 1891–1991: A History*, eBook (Metropolitan Books, 2014)

19 Lenin, V.I. and Gregory Zinoviev, *Socialism and War*, eBook (1915)

20 Lenin, V. I., 'Second Letter: The New Government and the Proletariat', *Letters From Afar,* eBook (March 1917, OS)

21 A method of transport that moves internationally without its contents being legally recognised as having entered or left the nations in question.

22 Lenin, V.I., *April Theses*, 7 April 1917 (OS). The *April Theses* were first announced in a speech in two meetings on 4 April 2017 (OS) and were subsequently published in the Bolshevik newspaper *Pravda*.

23 Pearson, Michael, *The Sealed Train: Journey to Revolution, Lenin, 1917* (Readers Union, 1975), p.126

24 Ibid, p.134

25 Lenin, V.I., 'Speech on the Attitude Towards the Provisional Government', 2nd All-Russia Congress of Soviets of Workers and Soldiers, June 1917, www.marxists. org/archive/lenin/works/1917/jul/07.htm

26 Lenin, V.I., 'The Political Situation', 23 July 1917 (OS), www.marxists.org/archive/ lenin/works/1917/jul/10b.htm

27 Lenin, V.I., 'A Letter to the Central Committee and the Petrograd and Moscow Committees of the RSDLP', 16 September 1917 (OS); from Sebestyen, Victor, Lenin the Dictator (Weidenfeld & Nicolson, 2017), p.337

28 Years later (after the creation of the USSR) official propaganda led many people to believe that the October Revolution had been quite violent but, in reality, it was fairly bloodless (although a Bolshevik-controlled naval cruiser did open fire on the Provisional Government's offices at the Winter Palace).

29 Trotsky, Leon, in an outburst during the All-Russian Soviet Congress, Petrograd, 24 October 1917 (OS), *from* Sebestyen, *Lenin the Dictator*, p.22

30 Lenin, V.I., in a speech during the All-Russian Soviet Congress, Petrograd, 24 October 1917 (OS), www.marxists.org/archive/lenin/works/1917/oct/25-26/index.htm

31 Trotsky, Leon, *The History of the Russian Revolution* (1930). Translated by Max Eastman, 1932, eBook.

32 Laver, John, *Personalities & Powers: Lenin – Liberator or Oppressor?* (Hodder Education, 1994)

33   Darby, Graham, *The Russian Revolution: Tsarism to Bolshevism, 1861–1924* (Longman, 1998), p.98

34   Sebestyen, *Lenin the Dictator*, p.22

35   Reed, John, *Ten Days That Shook the World* (Penguin, 1977).

LENIN'S RUSSIA
1917–24

This chapter will examine:

2.1: The role of Lenin and the relative importance of various factors – such as Red Terror – that contributed to the Bolshevik victory in the Civil War.

2.2: The role of Trotsky, the strengths of the Bolsheviks and the weaknesses of the Whites during the civil war.

2.3: The reasons for the introduction of the three main Bolshevik economic policies – State Capitalism, War Communism, and the New Economic Policy – and their different aspects between 1917 and 1924.

2.4: How successful Lenin was in achieving his economic aims for Russia by 1924 and the problems that he faced in this period.

2.5: The role of women and the family, as well as the position of the Church, popular culture and the arts.

At the end of this chapter there will be a summary of the causes and effects of some of the key events in this period, along with some exam-style questions.

2.1: Lenin's Consolidation of Power and Civil War, 1917–21

Key dates and events, 1917–24

1917	24–25 October	The October Revolution – the Bolshevik seizure of power.
	2 December	Armistice agreed with Germany.
1918	6 January	Bolshevik regime locks members of Constituent Assembly out of the Tauride Palace, where it had met for only one day.
	1 February	Russia finally adopts the Gregorian (New Style/NS) Calendar.
	23 February	Red Army is founded
	3 March	Treaty of Brest-Litovsk signed.
	12 March	Moscow becomes the new capital of Russia.
	8 April	Trotsky made Commissar for War.
	8 June	'War Communism' adopted.
	1 September	The Red Terror begins
1921	7–17 March	Trotsky puts down the Kronstadt Rebellion
	21 March	The NEP replaces 'War Communism'.
1922	16 April	The Treaty of Rapallo is signed between Russia and Germany.
	3 April	Stalin becomes general secretary of the Communist Party.
	30 December	The Union of Soviet Socialist Republics (USSR) is established.
1924	21 January	Lenin dies.

Problems facing Lenin's new government in November 1917

The success of Trotsky's planned revolution had shocked many, and it seemed unlikely that the world's first Communist state would last for more than a few months. Having taken power, Lenin and his party faced a number of significant and pressing problems, including:

- The future of the Constituent Assembly
- The removal of political opposition within Russia
- The creation of a socialist state
- The consolidation of political power
- Gaining control of the whole country

- The First World War
- The opposition of other countries to the establishment of the workers' state
- The threat of civil war
- Economic problems
- The creation of a socialist economy
- Discontent among peasants
- The lack of heavy industry
- A backward and inefficient agricultural sector
- Limited support for the Bolsheviks, outside Petrograd and Moscow
- The Bolsheviks' lack of administrative experience

Lenin's early political problems, November 1917–March 1921

Lenin claimed that the October Revolution was orchestrated by the soviets and that its aim was the creation of a workers' republic, but in reality, power had been seized by a small group of dedicated revolutionaries and their position was less than secure. While the Bolsheviks may have dominated the soviets, the party enjoyed limited support outside the two main cities, Petrograd and Moscow.

The Bolsheviks could not prevent elections to the Constituent Assembly being held in November 1917. They won 9.8 million votes (23.5 per cent of the total cast in the election) and 23.9 per cent of the seats, while the Kadets (Constitutional Democrats) received 1.8 million votes. The Socialist Revolutionary Party (SRs), however, won 17.1 million votes (41 per cent of the total) and 54.1 per cent of the seats.[1]

Lenin had no desire to share power on a long-term basis with the SRs or any other party, as that would have forced him to compromise and dilute his Communist policies. So in his attempts to build a new state and see off any threats to it, he was relentless.

On 5 January, just as the Constituent Assembly was about to meet for the first (and only) time, Lenin ordered soldiers to open fire on pro-Constituent-Assembly demonstrators and to disperse the crowd. In spite of this, the Assembly convened at the Tauride Palace and even passed several resolutions (which Lenin completely ignored) but did so in a very threatening atmosphere. Armed Lenin supporters had been placed throughout the building and even in the debating chamber. The next day, the palace was locked and surrounded by Red Guards. Delegates found it impossible to enter. Lenin then announced that the Assembly had been dissolved.

Lenin attempted to justify his actions by saying that, not only had the SRs and Kadets rigged the Constituent Assembly elections in their favour, a revolutionary government, supposedly taking its authority from the soviets, had already been created by the October Revolution. In his opinion, there was clearly no need for a process of constitutional reform to continue. Instead, he intended for the All-Russian Congress of Soviets to be the country's supreme governing body, with the Sovnarkom ('Soviet Council of People's Commissars') as the executive council. The Sovnarkom had been set up in November 1917, in the wake of the October Revolution, with Lenin as chairman, and it would supervise and issue instructions to state bodies.

Russia in the First World War: the Treaty of Brest-Litovsk

The decision to continue an unpopular war had helped to undermine the Provisional Government and boost support for the Bolsheviks, so it is no surprise that, in December 1917, revolutionary Russia and Germany signed an armistice agreement, bringing hostilities to an end and paving the way for a peace treaty. After all, Germany had also helped Lenin to return to Russia and, even after Lenin had taken power, continued to support the Bolsheviks financially.

Russia's former allies, namely Britain and France, were already very suspicious of the world's first Communist state, and were horrified at the country's withdrawal from the conflict.[2] But Lenin was keen to end Russia's participation in, what he had called, "an imperialist war", and gave the role of chief negotiator to Trotsky[3] – who had been made commissar for foreign affairs on 8 November 1917 as part of the new system of revolutionary government.

Trotsky (along with other leading Bolsheviks) tried to prolong the negotiations being held in Brest-Litovsk, as part of a strategy he described as "neither war nor peace!"[4] He had hoped that Russia would not need to agree to the harsh terms being proposed: that the German forces would collapse and that an international revolution, inspired by the success in Russia, would spread across Western Europe. Field Marshal Hindenburg, who led the German delegation, found this approach very frustrating, complaining that Trotsky and Lenin behaved as if they had won the war, when in reality they had been forced to seek peace terms with Germany.

On 9 February 1918, Germany signed a separate peace treaty with the government of the (German-supported) Ukrainian People's Republic, thereby putting more pressure on Lenin to do a deal. By the third week of

February 1918, the Germans had grown tired of the Bolsheviks' delaying tactics and briefly resumed their Eastern offensive. Lenin's new government was in danger of being overthrown.

Lenin told Trotsky that they would have to accept what was on offer. The Germans, who had clearly succeeded in scaring the Bolsheviks, halted their advance on 23 February and re-iterated their harsh peace terms. Trotsky recognised that the Treaty of Brest-Litovsk was a terrible deal for Russia – in private he described it as a German "diktat" – but ultimately he and the other Bolsheviks regarded themselves as "international revolutionaries" and their loyalty was not to Russia as a nation, but to the expected worldwide global proletarian revolution they predicted after their success in October 1917.[5]

On 3 March, the Russians signed the treaty. Lenin, realising that further conflict was a possibility, made Moscow the new capital of Russia only nine days later, on 12 March.

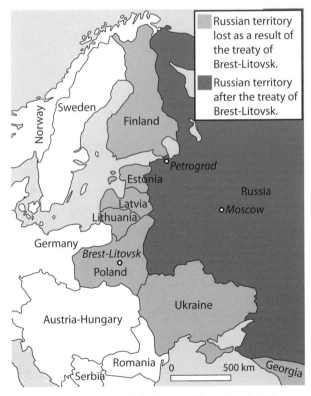

Russian territory lost in the Treaty of Brest-Litovsk, 1918.

Most historians agree that Lenin had little choice but to accept the terms of the Treaty of Brest-Litovsk, but the terms were undoubtedly severe. Russia lost 32 per cent of its agricultural land; large areas of its European territory; 75 per cent of its coal and iron-ore mines; 33 per cent of its factories; 26 per cent of its railway network; and more than 60 million people.[6] But Lenin's pragmatic decision to withdraw from the First World War helped the Bolshevik regime to remain in political power after 1918, and that, after all, was his main objective: the survival of the Bolshevik state at any price.

GROUP ACTIVITY

As a group, look at the problems facing Lenin and the Bolsheviks immediately after the October Revolution. Think about:

- Immediate political problems
- Immediate economic problems
- Long-term problems
- External problems

Discuss and present your findings.

CONSOLIDATE YOUR KNOWLEDGE

1. Why were the Bolsheviks in a politically weak position in November 1917?
2. Why was the Constituent Assembly a threat to Lenin?
3. How did Lenin deal with the Constituent Assembly?
4. What was the Sovnarkom?
5. Why was the First World War a major problem for Lenin's new government?
6. What were the aims of the German delegates at the peace conference?
7. Why did Trotsky object to the terms of the Treaty of Brest-Litovsk?
8. Why did Lenin support the signing of the Treaty in March 1918?
9. How did the terms of the Treaty of Brest-Litovsk affect Russia in March 1918?

Lenin and the Civil War, 1918–21

After the Treaty of Brest-Litovsk had been signed, there was a backlash against the Bolshevik leadership Many people (including some Bolsheviks) were angry about the terms agreed. Some members of the smaller, 'left' (i.e. pro-Bolshevik) faction of the SRs had formed an uneasy coalition with the Bolsheviks after the October Revolution, but on 15 March 1918, after Lenin had made peace with Germany, the few remaining SRs in the revolutionary government resigned. On the one hand, this meant that the Bolsheviks were now in control of all Russian state institutions, on the other, the government was now in a very weak political position. In fact, it looked as if it might not last long enough to celebrate the first anniversary of the October Revolution.

It could also be said that Lenin's government was bound by dogma and ignored political reality – an example of which is the establishment of the Comintern (better known as the Communist International) in March 1919. The Comintern was set up to encourage a worldwide Communist revolution: Communists from across all countries would come to Moscow to be trained as future leaders of their countries. It would prove to be ineffective under Lenin.

In March 1918, the new regime faced hostility from opponents of Bolshevism within Russia, including monarchists, militarists, and, for a short time, foreign nations (namely the Western powers, who didn't want Russia to withdraw from the war, and were, in any case, highly suspicious of violent revolutionary socialists). Collectively, these anti-Bolshevik forces were known as the Whites. They were politically divided in several ways but they had at least one thing in common: they wanted to remove Lenin and his followers (the Reds) from power. And so, in early 1918 a civil war developed between these two groups, the Reds and the Whites: a civil war that the Bolsheviks would win in 1921, thanks to Lenin's forward planning.

In December 1917, he had established a secret police organisation, the Cheka, whose actions were often so extreme that they often shocked or disgusted even Bolshevik supporters. Lenin oversaw some of the Cheka's operations personally and, from his office in the Kremlin, could be just as cold-blooded as the murderous officers on the ground.

Lenin was also a prime mover behind the Sovnarkom's decision, late in January 1918, to establish the Red Army, which came into being in February.[7] Trotsky – in a new role as commissar for war – was given full control in

March, the same month, incidentally, that the peace treaty with Germany was signed. Lenin, fearing that the peace might not last, moved the seat of government to the Kremlin, the old citadel at the heart of Moscow.

By the summer of 1918, civil war had spread across Russia. Lenin, determined to maintain his grip on power by any means necessary, reacted with a series of ruthless measures:

- Leading members of other Russian political parties, who hadn't already been driven into exile, were arrested.

- The tsar and members of his immediate family were killed by the Bolsheviks in Ekaterinburg in July 1918. Lenin wanted to stop them being rescued by anti-Bolshevik forces and used as figureheads by any rival, White government, which might then be recognised as the legitimate government of Russia by other countries.

- In August 1918, he started to challenge the 'kulaks' (property-owning peasants)when they resisted War Communism (a series of tough economic policies introduced by Lenin in June 1918 [see p.77]). In the 'hanging telegram' to the Bolshevik chiefs in Penza Province, Lenin said, "Comrades, the kulak uprising in your five districts must be crushed without pity. The interests of the whole revolution demand it … An example must be made. Hang not less than 100 known kulaks … publish their names … identify hostages …
PS Find tougher people."[8]

On 30 August 1918, there was an attempt on Lenin's life in Moscow, and Petrograd's Cheka commander was assassinated on the same day. Both events were used to justify the launch of the Red Terror – a campaign of threats, beatings, executions, starvation, arson, mass surveillance, interrogation, torture and propaganda – on the first week of September. In October 1920 Lenin justified his actions:

Whoever does not understand the need for dictatorship of any revolutionary class to secure its victory, understands nothing of the history of revolution … The scientific term 'dictatorship' means nothing more nor less than authority untrammeled by any laws, absolutely unrestricted by any rules whatever, and based directly on force.[9]

Lenin would go on to use the Cheka to force an often reluctant Russian population (peasants in particular) to comply with the harsh requirements of

War Communism – which Lenin thought necessary for a Bolshevik victory in the civil war [see p.77] – and he fully supported the savage tactics they employed.

By March 1921, the civil war had swung dramatically in the Bolsheviks' favour: they had defeated the Whites and dealt with the threat of foreign intervention [covered in section 2.2]. Under Lenin's single-minded leadership, the Bolshevik one-party "workers' state" had survived.

The Red Army and the Cheka had obeyed Lenin's orders without question and ensured victory through their use of Red Terror, while Trotsky, too, had been key in winning the civil war. He had proven himself to be an able administrator and military commander, and had taken full advantage of the disorganisation of the Whites, who were divided into several (uncooperative) factions, and who were without adequate support and supplies from 'friendly' foreign governments.

Lenin addresses a crowd in Moscow, 1920. Kamenev and Trotsky can be seen on the steps of the podium.

CONSOLIDATE YOUR KNOWLEDGE

10. Give two reasons for the outbreak of civil war in Russia, during the early part of 1918.

11. List three measures taken by Lenin between December 1917 and March 1918 that helped the Bolsheviks prepare for civil war.

12. Explain how these measures enabled the Bolsheviks to win the civil war.

13. Explain why the Bolsheviks used Red Terror.

14. Explain how Lenin justified his political actions between 1918 and March 1921.

15. What had Lenin achieved politically by March 1921?

16. Explain how the Cheka helped to secure the Bolsheviks state by 1921.

17. Explain how Lenin acted ruthlessly between 1918 and 1921.

TASK

Using your own knowledge and research, explain how Lenin's leadership helped the Bolsheviks win the civil war. Discuss and present your findings.

2.2: Trotsky and the Whites in the Civil War, 1918–21

Trotsky and the Red Army, 1918–21

The Bolsheviks' preparations for the seemingly inevitable civil war had begun in early 1918. In February, Trotsky had overseen the creation of the Red Army and in March, despite having never served in the armed forces or received any formal military training, he was made commissar of war, essentially giving him full responsibility for the prosecution of the civil war. He believed that the civil war was necessary to maintain the revolution, declaring to the Petrograd Soviet, "Our party is for civil war … civil war in the name of direct and ruthless struggle against counter-revolutionaries."[10]

In the second half of 1918, when the civil war intensified, Trotsky began to transform the Red Army into a war machine. In June 1918, with many urban workers already in uniform, Trotsky introduced conscription and forced reluctant peasants (from areas under Bolshevik control) to defend the Revolution too. By 1919, the Red Army had approximately three million men. By 1920, it had a total strength of more than five million men, and Trotsky had shown that he was a rousing and skilful commander-in-chief, often leading from the front and travelling in his famous armoured train from one unit to the next to boost morale.

Many of the conscripted peasants were not inclined to join the army, however, and there were a significant number of deserters, especially at harvest time. Trotsky used special punitive brigades, run by the Cheka, and the Red Guards (the original and loyal Bolshevik military units that had existed before the establishment of the Red Army) to deal with deserters and so-called 'enemies of the state' (people accused of opposition to the Bolsheviks) within the army. He introduced a system of military discipline that included execution for deserters and those who refused to follow orders.[11] Fear created obedience and helped to create an army that would fight enemies of the Bolshevik state without question.

Trotsky had wanted a disciplined, well-trained, and adequately equipped army, and he knew he needed the advice of professional soldiers, so he insisted on the replacement of ramshackle and amateurish Bolshevik forces with an experienced professional general staff. Although many Bolsheviks were strongly against the idea, during the summer of 1918 he recruited approximately 50,000 former officers from the pre-Revolutionary Tsarist army. Their knowledge and experience was invaluable, both in guiding the new Red Army while it was fighting the Whites, and in training the millions of conscripts who, from June 1918 onwards, were drafted into it.

Trotsky employed two very effective methods for controlling these former officers of the Imperial Russian army. Firstly, a political commissar (political leader) was assigned to every unit in the Red Army to act as the government's eyes and ears. The political commissar had to approve any orders proposed by the commander he was monitoring, and was of an equivalent rank or position of authority. Secondly, to prevent defections to the Whites, desertion or displays of disloyalty, many officers' families were held as hostages by either the Cheka, or the more fanatical Bolsheviks.

Trotsky inspects some of the Red Army's special brigades.

Trotsky felt that this extreme action was necessary to ensure loyalty in an extreme situation and Lenin, who feared that the Bolsheviks might be driven from power, gave his full support, brushing aside the criticism some party members had of Trotsky's methods. Trotsky's reputation for bravery and decisiveness (a reputation helped by his frequent train trips to the front lines) boosted the Red Army's morale.

Trotsky, now the 'people's commissar for army and naval affairs' (effectively the defence minister), had also proposed reforms of a more practical nature. In April 1918 he had set up a departmental sub-committee to look into such matters as uniform and rank. In the days of the Red Guards and first few months of the Red Army, initially comprised of volunteers, there had been no military ranks.[12] Every soldier was a 'Red Army Man' and officers, elected by soldiers, were 'Red Commanders'. Trotsky's sub-committee had its recommendations approved by Russia's Central Executive Committee on 29 November and a rank structure was re-established in the armed forces.

By the beginning of 1921, the Red Army was well on the way to defeating White forces, thanks partly to Trotsky's widespread army reforms. As historian Robert Service put it, "Trotsky's brilliance had been proved before 1918. What took everyone aback was his organisational capacity and ruthlessness as he transformed the Red Army into a fighting force."[13]

CONSOLIDATE YOUR KNOWLEDGE

1. Outline Trotsky's political achievements before 1918.
2. Why did some Bolshevik leaders believe, by the early part of 1918, that a Civil War would be politically necessary?
3. How did Trotsky greatly increase the size of the Red Army by 1920? Why did he need to do that?
4. Name two military reforms that Trotsky introduced, in order to make the Red Army an effective fighting force.
5. Why did some Bolsheviks oppose the use of former Tsarist army officers being appointed as Red Army officers?
6. Why were political commissars brought into the Red Army?
7. What other measures did Trotsky introduce in order to make the Red Army more effective?

The strengths of the Reds

The contrast between the Bolshevik position in January 1918 to that of March 1921 could hardly have been greater. By early 1921 the former enemies of Bolshevism were in headlong retreat or had already been defeated. Most of the foreign military contingents had been withdrawn since 1919. Only a few remote regions, far from Moscow, were not under total Bolshevik control. Victory by 1921 owed much to Trotsky's efforts and leadership – both in politics and in the military.

Trotsky's aims were to disrupt the supply networks of the anti-Bolshevik forces and keep them as divided by geography as they were by political views and allegiance. His success in meeting those goals was assisted by the strengths of his own party:

- There was a good deal of unity within the party and it was reinforced by Lenin's strong leadership, while the Red Army had become a very capable instrument of war.

- War Communism [see p.77] had helped to feed the troops (although it had caused discontent among some groups of sailors and peasants, and thereby created another threat to the regime's survival).

Trotsky was an inspirational military leader and an able and creative administrator who had a good working relationship with Lenin. Mutual trust and respect existed between the two men, and Lenin gave Trotsky his full support throughout the civil war – defending him to those in the party, like Stalin, who still distrusted him.

CONSOLIDATE YOUR KNOWLEDGE

8. What were the strengths of the Bolshevik's position in March 1918?
9. To what extent had Trotsky achieved his civil war aims by 1921?
10. Give three reasons for supporting the view that Trotsky's role was decisive in determining the outcome of the civil war.

GROUP ACTIVITY

Organise a class debate with the motion:

"Without Trotsky the Bolsheviks would not have won the Civil War."

Economic, geographic and geopolitical factors

In the middle of 1918 the main Bolshevik military forces were concentrated in a fairly small area (relative to the size of Russia as a whole). Fortunately for the Bolsheviks, this area contained Petrograd and Moscow, the most populous and industrialised cities in Russia, and so they were able to control the important parts of the railway network and most centres of manufacturing. War Communism backed by the continuing Red Terror [see p.60] meant a restructuring of the economy (in areas under Bolshevik control), and it played a significant part in ensuring that the Red Army could obtain food, personnel and other things needed to carry on fighting. The resultant war economy that was created (on the Bolshevik side of the conflict) made a transformation of Bolshevik political fortunes possible.

From the outset, Trotsky's priorities were to keep industry and communications under Bolshevik control, and defend the areas they already held. An advantage of holding the smaller area was that it was easier to control. The vast tracts of land held by the Whites may have looked impressive on a map but those areas tended to be bleak, sparsely populated and had little economic development or modern communication systems.

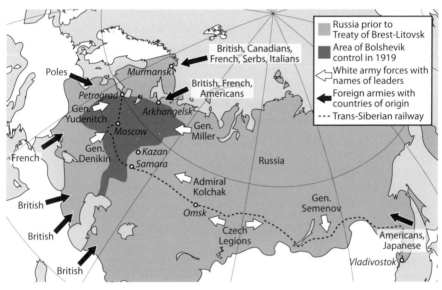

Land under Bolshevik control, 1919. The Bolshevik government controlled about one eighth of post-First-World-War Russia when the Civil War began in the middle of 1918.

At one stage, Lenin had contemplated a withdrawal from Petrograd as the city was at times almost encircled by anti-Bolshevik forces. It was probably only Trotsky's energetic insistence that they hold on to a site of such strategic and symbolic importance (after all, this had been the location of the Revolution) that prevented it being taken by the Whites. Trotsky travelled to Petrograd and assumed personal responsibility for the improvement of its defences (a task that regional governor Gregory Zinoviev seemed to have handled badly).

On a wider scale, the First World War was still having an impact on Russian affairs. In April 1918, Germany landed an entire army division in Finland to aid the White anti-Communist side in the Finnish Civil War.[14] Finland, largely self-governing throughout two centuries of Russian sovereignty, had declared complete independence from Russia on 6 December 1917. The Finnish Whites were victorious as early as May 1918, largely due to German assistance.

Between 1915 and 1917, the Allies had supplied the Tsarist government, and the Provisional Government which succeeded it, with large quantities of materiel, in the (ultimately vain) hope that the Eastern Front would be kept open. With some of its troops now in Finland and the Baltic states, the danger was that Germany might cut the supply lines between northern Russian ports (principally Murmansk and Archangel) and the interior of the country. It might even seize the ports themselves (along with the military equipment and other supplies stockpiled there).

It was under these circumstances that the Allies decided to intervene in the Russian Civil War, though they were reluctant to engage in direct combat with the Red Army. A naval blockade of Russia was imposed, with the aim of restricting imports of weapons and other useful items by the Bolsheviks.

With this, Lenin and Trotsky realised that, for the Red Army to be successful in the civil war, suitable quantities of weapons, munitions and other military equipment would have to be produced in Russia: fortunately for them, the Bolsheviks controlled the parts of Russia which contained most of its factories and a very large percentage of its population.

CONSOLIDATE YOUR KNOWLEDGE

11. Why did Trotsky feel that the Bolsheviks should not abandon Petrograd?
12. Why were the parts of Russia which were controlled by the Bolsheviks so important, economically?
13. How had economic factors helped the Bolsheviks to achieve success in the civil war by March 1921?
14. Why did the Allies get involved in the Russian Civil War?

Railways and other communication systems

In general, the parts of Russia held by the Bolsheviks in 1918 were much more economically developed than those of their opponents. The Bolsheviks controlled areas with the densest network of railway lines, the busiest junctions, and most of the marshalling yards, locomotive depots and engineering workshops. Thus they were able to keep their railways running and Trotsky was able to distribute soldiers, weapons, ammunition and other military supplies to his front-line formations much more effectively than the enemy.

Trotsky appreciated the strategic usefulness of railways. He could move reinforcements at a reasonable speed (and often at short notice) towards almost any region if it was threatened by White forces. The railways were also useful ways in which to distribute supplies and spread Bolshevik propaganda.

Another great asset which the Bolsheviks had at their disposal were electrically-powered communications networks, namely telephone lines and, more importantly, the two systems on which messages could be sent (in Morse code) over long distances. These were telegraph lines (often run by the railway) and wireless (or radio) telegraphy.

When the Red Army had grown stronger, its cavalry units were able to trek across country and harass White forces. That made control of an isolated stretch of railway line by the Whites less important than it may have seemed. Railway lines in White areas could be damaged and were sometimes difficult to repair because of a lack of manpower or lack of materials. Rolling stock was scarce and locomotives scarcer still.

TASK

Copy the table below and give examples of how each strength helped the Bolsheviks during the Civil War.

Bolshevik strengths during the Civil War	Examples
Role of Trotsky	
Role of Lenin	
Economic factors	
Railways and communications	
Geographic factors	

The weaknesses of the Whites

When the civil war erupted in the middle of 1918, the new Bolshevik state was seriously threatened by White forces and their foreign allies, mainly in the in the north, north-east and south-west of Russia.

However, White forces were scattered geographically and divided politically. A loose coalition of socialists, liberals, conservatives and some non-Russian nationalities from within the boundaries of pre-Revolutionary Russia, their only common aim was the overthrow of the Communist government they feared and hated. Their slogan was "Russia, one and indivisible", but as the war progressed, the various White groups were often unable to set aside their differences and their slogan became somewhat ironic.

Among the disparate elements of the White movement, the majority were supporters of reform-minded groups such as the Mensheviks and SRs. A small percentage of Whites were conservative (opposed to radical social or economic change) and wanted the old-style Tsarist system to be brought back, while a slightly larger number (though still constituting a small minority of the overall movement) wanted a constitutional monarchy to be established and run along British lines. Some of the latter hoped that a more enlightened and sensible member of the Romanov dynasty (probably Nicholas's brother, Grand Duke Michael) could be persuaded to sit on the throne.

On top of this, most of the non-Russian nationalities of the former Russian Empire had backed the anti-Bolsheviks, but by February 1918 most of these nations had declared independence. This led to clashes among the few Russian White leaders who wanted to hold on to the territory of the old Tsarist Empire and those who were prepared to consider new constitutional arrangements.

Then there was the issue of leadership Although some White commanders showed flashes of brilliance, none of the leaders had the same sort of presence or following as the Red leaders. As the historian Robert Service put it, "No White leaders had the imagination and ruthlessness of Trotsky, Lenin or Stalin."[15] In addition, the military leaders of the Whites, such as Admiral Alexander Kolchak (the commander-in-chief of White forces) and Anton Denikin (another leading White general), were often geographically divided with little coordination of their armies. Kolchak, for instance was based in Omsk, a Siberian city 2,700 km from Moscow while Denikin started out east of the Crimea and pushed northwards towards Moscow but his advance stalled about 400 km short of his main objective.[16]

Generally, there was a lack of overall strategy. At times, the main White army groups all appeared to be fighting separate wars, and tactics were often poor. In several cases, White forces had to retreat during operations that had initially been very successful, because supply lines had been stretched to breaking point or because long, thin columns of troops had become vulnerable to attack from the Reds.

Even at a local level there were problems. Some White units (such as the Czechoslovak Legion[17]) displayed great bravery and made breathtaking progress but overall the White army tended to be unreliable and poorly disciplined. Many refused to obey orders, while some were responsible for brutality and even massacres. Members of minority groups (notably Jews) were particularly affected by White pogroms. The White army was outnumbered by the Reds, but White leaders found it difficult to enforce conscription. Peasants were worried that, if the Whites were victorious in the civil war, any land they had taken for themselves would be returned to the ownership of the aristocracy and gentry.

Peasants came to see the Reds as the lesser of two evils and the Bolsheviks' (very effective) anti-White propaganda played on such fears. It accused the Whites of being unpatriotic – due to the association with foreign governments and 'reactionary' Russians – and of attempting to bring back the Tsarist system. Conversely, non-Russian nationalities started to lose confidence in a movement that seemed to place too much emphasis on the Russian national identity. The Whites lost popular support across parts of Russia – its propaganda efforts were no match for those of the Bolsheviks. The movement struggled to retain, let alone gain, popular support.

As Peter Struve, a former Duma politician, stated after the Civil War, "The Whites conducted themselves as if nothing had happened, whereas in reality the whole world around them had collapsed."[18]

CONSOLIDATE YOUR KNOWLEDGE

15. In which parts of Russia were White forces based, in 1918?
16. Name two geographical disadvantages that the Whites faced.
17. Which groups supported the White movement? List the chief aims of each of these groups.
18. Outline the main weaknesses of the Whites' military forces.
19. Why did the Whites lose the support of these groups?
20. Why did the peasants mistrust the Whites?
21. Why was White propaganda less successful than that of the Reds?

Foreign intervention and its effects

When Russia signed the peace treaty with Germany in March 1918, the Allied nations were far from pleased. They were horrified by Bolshevism and shocked by the Revolution but expected the new regime in Petrograd to collapse within months, if not weeks.

When the civil war broke out, early in the summer of 1918, Allied armies (British, Indian, Canadian, Australian, French, American, Italian, Greek and Japanese) began to devise ways of assisting the Whites – though the picture was complicated a little by the military presence, until 1918, of the Central Powers (chiefly Germany) in the Baltic States, Finland, Romania, Poland and the Ukraine.

By the end of 1918, there were tens of thousands of Allied troops in Russia, and the Bolsheviks were able to present themselves to the people as patriots, defending Mother Russia against foreign invaders. Allied blockades (along with the Bolshevik control of territory at Moscow and Petrograd) made the Whites dependent on the Allies for supplies of arms and equipment.

However, once the First World War had come to an end (and especially after the peace treaties had been signed in Paris in the summer and early autumn of 1919), Russia's problems seemed to be much less important to war-weary Western governments than they had been between 1914 and 1918. Germany had been defeated and it was no longer necessary to tie down German forces in Eastern Europe. By the end of 1919, foreign aid to the Whites had almost dried up, although a few units (notably Japanese ones) stayed on Russian territory for much longer.

In the end, the Allies had provided only limited support to the Whites, and the price paid for this was higher than expected. The presence of foreign troops had damaged the White cause, drained it of much popular support, and created an image problem that had left it weaker, by 1921, than it had been at the beginning of the conflict. In some ways, foreign intervention was more of a liability than the asset some Whites (and foreign governments) had expected.

CONSOLIDATE YOUR KNOWLEDGE

22. Why did some foreign countries dispatch military forces to help the Whites?

23. Which countries sent troops and/or warships to help the Whites?

24. Describe the way in which the Bolsheviks were able to discredit the White armies.

25. Why had most foreign troops left Russia by 1920?

Reasons for the failure of the Whites

All in all, there was a marked contrast between the circumstances of the White forces and those of the Red Army. The Whites had some major weaknesses that, in 1921, led to their defeat:

- *Geographical factors and poor supply lines*
  - White units were often based in remote or inhospitable places and sometimes lacked the means to receive necessary supplies.
  - They were spread around Russia, with little regard for strategy, and isolated from each other physically.

- *Political divisions*
  - The White movement was divided into different groups, which found it difficult to cooperate with each other for ideological, bureaucratic or personal divisions.

- *Military weaknesses*
  - Unreliable food supplies and limited munitions imports.
  - They were outnumbered by the Reds.
  - Some units lacked discipline.
  - Difficulty in enforcing conscription.

- *Inadequacies of foreign intervention.*
- *Their communications (as well as their logistics) were often poor.*
- *Lack of popular support.*
- *Lack of strong, central leadership*

TASK

Create a spider diagram that lists the reasons for the failure of the Whites in the civil war by 1921. Which of these was the most important in your opinion?

2.3: Bolshevik Economic Policies, 1917–24

During the war, millions of peasants were displaced and agricultural production steadily declined. The Provisional Government did not introduce any land reforms, increasing rural unrest and discontent. Factories weren't able to operate normally and industrial production suffered. The Provisional Government had failed to tackle Russia's economic problems with their limited economic reforms, and by October 1917, Russia was facing economic collapse.

Like most Bolshevik leaders, Lenin was a political theorist, not an expert on economics, and he had little experience of administration or finance. Yet, under his leadership, Russia had three different (and contrasting) sets of economic policies: State Capitalism, (1917–18); War Communism, (1918–21); and the NEP, (1921–28). He used propaganda to explain his economic objectives to the Russian people and his messages were often delivered through articles written for the Bolshevik newspaper *Pravda* (the Russian word for truth) or through revolutionary posters.

In this section, the aims, features and effects of each set of policies will be examined, with a look at how each policy was influenced by individuals, ideology and external factors.

State Capitalism, 1917–18

Aims of State Capitalism

After the Bolsheviks had been in power for three months the Sovnarkom cancelled foreign debts, and indeed all government debts from the Tsar's Russian Empire and the Provisional Government. This led to the introduction to the first of Lenin's three economic policies, State Capitalism, which lasted from late 1917 until June 1918.

According to Marxist theory, State Capitalism is a transitory stage, on the way to full-blown socialism. Under this system, government bodies (not workers) assume ownership of most profit-making organisations, and small businesses are left in private hands. A truly socialist system would follow and, in it, everyone would be equal. The workers would control the means of producing, distributing and exchanging wealth (most of which are, in a capitalist system, controlled by a mixture of private individuals and private corporations).

At this time, the Bolsheviks were trying to stabilise and reinforce their position of political power. They regarded State Capitalism as a stop-gap: a temporary fix that would be replaced by, what they saw as, a truly socialist economy. Lenin hoped that State Capitalism (aided by propaganda, of course) would make the new regime more popular, while giving the Bolsheviks the power to restructure the economy, to suit their ideology. He felt that it was the most suitable approach to the problems of a country in which privately owned small businesses – either small family firms (very few of which were limited companies) or sole traders – accounted for the bulk of economic activity.

Although many Bolshevik leaders came from middle-class backgrounds, they frequently condemned or derided the middle classes. However, the new government now depended on the cooperation of most sections of the bourgeoisie (and not merely on that of shopkeepers and tradesmen), in order to make a transition to State Capitalism. Lenin knew that this transition was bound to take months, if not years.

On 5 December 1917, the Supreme Council of the National Economy (the Vesenkha) was established to assume overall direction of the Russian economy. The Vesenkha's influence was limited, but the body was able to oversee the nationalisation of Russia's banks and its railways.

On learning that large-scale industry was to be nationalised, some workers took matters into their own hands. They seemed to believe that the socialist system (about which many of them had read in Marxist pamphlets) was just around the corner. Without the authority of the Bolshevik government, groups of workers seized control of many factories from the owners.

Regardless of Marxist theory, Bolsheviks saw State Capitalism as necessary while they consolidated their authority. They had many enemies, were not in a very strong position, and the survival of the new regime was their main concern.

Features of State Capitalism

State Capitalism was implemented through a series of decrees, issued by Lenin's government. The two most important dealt with the two groups that were vital to the economy and to the survival of the Bolshevik regime – peasants and industrial workers.

The Land Decree was passed on 26 October 1917 by the All-Russian Congress of Soviets, the nearest thing that Bolshevik Russia had to a parliament. The decree abolished the right of private individuals and corporations to hold land. Large farms and private country estates (including those which belonged to the Church) were to be confiscated and their assets placed under the control of peasants' committees. Instead they were to be run as 'model farms'. Many peasants had already seized land from their landowners before the October Revolution and Lenin was trying to regularise or legalise the situation. To his opponents, both inside and outside Russia, he was merely condoning illegal action.

The Decree on Workers' Control (the draft of which appeared in *Pravda* on 3 November 1917, only one week after the Revolution), was passed on 14 November 1917 and published the following day. It supposedly gave workers control "of production, purchase and sale of products and raw materials, storage, and over business finances ... in all the sectors of industry, commerce, banking, agriculture, transport, cooperatives, and all others who employ workers making a salary or doing domestic work."[19]

Workers were to exercise control through elected councils, unless the firm was so small that all its employees could just sit around a table and discuss the running of the business themselves. The local soviet was to oversee and be notified of the membership of every Workers' Council within its area, so that members could be disciplined if they abused their positions or neglected their duties.

Certain aspects of State Capitalism (primarily the Workers' Councils and the allocation of agricultural land for use by peasants) may have increased support for the Bolsheviks among some sections of society but the system, as a whole, was proving to be ineffective by early 1918. By that summer, the possibility of civil war loomed large over Lenin. This was a threat that he could not ignore and a conflict the Bolsheviks had to win if they wanted to survive. He realised that a new economic policy, one that would give the government almost total control of key resources, was needed urgently:

> It would be extremely stupid and absurdly Utopian to assume that the transformation from capitalism to socialism is possible without coercion and without dictatorship[20]

Many Bolsheviks were opposed to this policy on ideological grounds – as historian Robert Service notes, "They put their arguments against Lenin in terms of doctrine: in their opinion, he was offering a strategy that made too many compromises with capitalism. What they omitted to mention was that this strategy was simply unworkable."[21]

CONSOLIDATE YOUR KNOWLEDGE

1. Why did Lenin adopt the system known as State Capitalism?
2. What were the economic aims of State Capitalism?
3. What measures did Lenin take to try and bring the economy under Bolshevik control?
4. Why, even when State Capitalism was introduced, did Bolshevik leaders think that it should be temporary?
5. In practice, what were the weaknesses of State Capitalism?
6. Why was State Capitalism replaced, in June 1918, with a different set of economic policies?

War Communism, 1918–21

Aims of War Communism

The Bolsheviks launched their second economic policy, War Communism, on June 1918 with one simple purpose: to win the civil war. Their aim was to create a war economy.

At this time, food shortages were increasing and large numbers of people were leaving the cities for rural areas. Peasants were blamed for falling agricultural production. The Bolshevik government justified War Communism by saying it had to ensure that the population and the armed forces were provided with the basic supplies they needed.

There is no doubt that Lenin wanted to drive up productivity in factories and farms, however, there may have been another motive for introducing War Communism. By bringing most aspects of Russia's economic life – chiefly overseas trade, Russian businesses, the industrial labour force, agriculture and peasants – under state control, the Bolsheviks were able to tighten their grip on power. Although it must be remembered that, at this stage, large parts of Russia were still not under Bolshevik control and the country was generally still economically undeveloped.

In its implementation, War Communism was certainly harsh, and its policies were incredibly unpopular with some groups (such as peasants and the Kronstadt sailors), even some Bolsheviks were critical. But for the most part, the majority of Bolsheviks felt that it was right for their government to dominate and control the economy, arguing that War Communism was a socialist system in that it allowed Bolsheviks to put their ideas into practice.

Features of War Communism

The plan was for Russia to have a centralised, planned economy, which was to be achieved through the following:

- Trade with other countries was brought under the direct management of state bodies.
- Any businesses which had remained in private hands were nationalised.
- Private ownership of businesses was, in principle, abolished.
- Workers were supervised much more closely by state bodies. For example, strikes were, to all intents and purposes, banned.
- All major industries were nationalised.
- The railways were placed fully under government control.
- Rationing (of food and other necessities) was introduced.
- Surplus food was confiscated from peasants so that it could be redistributed among the rest of the population.

While State Capitalism had severely restricted strikes in areas of national importance, under War Communism, strikes became illegal. With the aim of improving productivity in factories, the Workers' Councils of the State Capitalism system were replaced by more orthodox management structures. However, managers now answered to official bodies of the Bolshevik state.

Hoping to increase agricultural production, on 14 May 1918, the Bolsheviks introduced a policy for grain requisitioning (also known as 'Food Dictatorship'), in which peasants were instructed to voluntarily donate any food that they didn't need. In reality, the Bolsheviks and the Red Army determined how much should be taken and used Red Terror to take it: a policy that Lenin fully supported. Grain and other produce was seized by units known as 'Special Punishment' brigades or squads, depending on their size. These units were comprised of party volunteers, Cheka officers and some Red Army soldiers (often ones who were fervent supporters of the Bolsheviks). Peasants could be left with meagre rations or nothing at all to eat.

Many of the peasants that resisted were murdered by the special punishment units. Many more peasants had food, household goods or personal effects, agricultural produce or livestock confiscated, or sometimes destroyed. Such people were left with nothing to live on after all their agricultural produce had been taken. It is believed that, by the early part of 1921, Bolshevik-induced famine in parts of Russia had claimed as many as five million victims.

Many tried to resist War Communism. In October 1920, Alexander Antonov – a radical member of the Left SRs – led a series of rebellions in the Tambov region, fewer than 300 miles from Moscow. By February 1921, his peasant army, had approximately 70,000 fighters, and they successfully defended the area against Bolshevik intrusions. The Tambov Rebellion, as it was to be called, lasted for several months and was one of the largest and best-organised peasant rebellions during the civil war. The Bolsheviks retaliated without mercy, using a combination of poison gas, executions, and imprisonment in concentration camps to quell the protestors, and resulting in the deaths of approximately 140,000 peasants.

Then, in February 1921, representatives of the sailors, soldiers and other workers from the Kronstadt naval base investigated complaints about poor conditions in Petrograd. They sent the government a list of demands, high on which was a call for an end to War Communism. On 1 and 2 March, meetings were held at Kronstadt, attended by a large number of sailors and soldiers: men who, in 1917, had been among the most fervent supporters of the Bolshevik cause, but who now operated under the slogan, "Soviets without Bolsheviks". The meetings developed into an uprising against the Bolshevik regime and on 7 March, Trotsky responded with a merciless attack, which lasted for eleven days with heavy losses on both sides. By 17 March, Trotsky had put down the rising and over 500 rebels were executed on the spot. Approximately 14,000 people were killed – over 11,000 were Red Army soldiers, and over 2,000 were rebels, executed after the rising – and over 5000 rebels were imprisoned or placed into exile.

Among the consequences of War Communism (and the economic and social conditions that had existed before and during this period) were several that the Bolsheviks had not foreseen: a large black market in goods emerged after 1918; and the urban workforce dramatically declined, halving the population of cities such as Petrograd and Moscow, between 1918 and 1921.

War Communism helped the Red Army to win the civil war but its effects on the economy, on Russian society and even on the Bolsheviks themselves were damaging.

The main effects of War Communism
- The output of factories was reduced.
- The output of farms was reduced, even though the most important aims of War Communism had been to increase agricultural production (especially of cereals such as wheat and maize) and to provide adequate stocks of food.

- Persistent hyperinflation made the Russian currency almost worthless.
- By the early part of 1921, the whole economy was teetering on the brink of collapse.
- There was a further decline in the populations of virtually all the cities and large towns under Bolshevik control.
- Millions of people died of starvation or famine-related disease.
- In early 1921, food rations in the major cities were reduced by one third.
- Red Terror, the violence meted out by the ruthless Cheka (and other fanatical supporters of the regime) was intensified.
- The policies of War Communism generated resentment, particularly among workers and the peasants, e.g. the Tambov and Kronstadt Rebellions.
- Support for the Bolsheviks among ordinary Russians (not just among victims of Red Terror) was reduced.

Conclusion

War Communism had been imposed on the Russian people, through the use of systemic violence and intimidation by the Cheka who extended state control over most parts of Russian lives. It seems that Lenin, who believed that the end had justified the means, had placed the emphasis on 'War' rather than 'Communism': a brutal war waged against people in rural areas.

By March 1921, the Bolsheviks had essentially won the civil war and could no longer justify the continuation of War Communism. It had brought widespread famine to some parts of Russia and it is estimated to have cost up to ten million lives. Its economic failures and its cruelty were making the new government more hated than any tsar in living memory had been (at least among some sections of society) and it had stirred sufficient discontent to threaten the stability of the Communist state.

So, when Trotsky's forces put down the Kronstadt Rebellion so ruthlessly in March 1921, even Lenin realised that something needed to change: to him the rising had "lit up reality like a flash of lightning".[22] Certainly the economic and social costs of War Communism to Russia (and the damage it had caused to the party's reputation) had been significant – it was time to introduce a new economic policy.

CONSOLIDATE YOUR KNOWLEDGE

7. Give two reasons why Lenin introduced War Communism in June 1918.

8. What were War Communism's two most important economic aims?

9. What were War Communism's two most important political aims?

10. Why did Lenin introduce requisitioning of grain?

11. Explain two of the effects of grain requisitioning.

12. Why was Red Terror used to impose War Communism on the Russian people?

13. What effects did War Communism have on industry and factory workers?

14. What role did the Cheka play, between June 1918 and March 1921?

15. Why did the Kronstadt Rebellion break out in March 1921?

16. How did the Bolshevik regime deal with the Kronstadt Rebellion?

17. Explain the three most economically important effects of War Communism by 1921?

18. To what extent was War Communism a successful economic policy by 1921?

The New Economic Policy (NEP), 1921–24

Lenin was convinced that Russia needed breathing space, a chance for the economy to recover, and in March 1921, during the 10th Congress of the All-Russian Communist Party (as it had been renamed in March 1918), he proposed that the New Economic Policy (NEP) be adopted as a short-term replacement for War Communism.

A number of high-ranking members, including Trotsky, wanted to retain and even intensify War Communism. They opposed the policy change, alleging that it was a retreat to capitalism and a betrayal of Marxist ideology, but Lenin, being slightly more pragmatic, saw the need for drastic action to reverse his economic policies. He forced the matter, and even managed to produce the appearance of unity by passing a law banning factionalism within the party, thereby stifling all debate. As he told the congress delegates, "We must try to satisfy the demands of the peasants".[23]

Reasons for the introduction of the NEP

- There was a need to regain the cooperation of industrial workers and peasants.
- By 1921, industrial workers in Moscow were protesting and striking over food shortages and reduced rations.
- In the early part of 1921, millions of peasants had starved to death because of a combination of War Communism, famine and disease.
- War Communism was despised by the peasantry and urban workers.
- Red Terror and the use of the Cheka had proved very unpopular.
- The Bolsheviks had been forced to suppress the Tambov Rebellion and the Kronstadt Rebellion.
- Agricultural production had fallen, even though one of War Communism's main aims had been to increase food supplies.
- Industrial output had also fallen dramatically by 1921.
- The civil war was effectively over and the White side had disintegrated.
- By 1921, the Russian economy as a whole had become much weaker.
- Discontent by 1921 now threatened the survival of the Bolshevik regime.

Main features of the NEP

- The ban on privately owned, profit-making enterprises was lifted.
- The state relaxed central economic planning a little but retained control of all major industries.
- Small-scale businesses (employing twenty people or fewer), were permitted.
- Grain requisitioning was replaced with a levy or tax on agricultural produce, which could be paid in kind (i.e. in the form of produce rather than money).
- Peasants were now allowed to keep or sell surplus food after meeting their quotas.

Like State Capitalism, the NEP was meant to be a temporary measure, but Lenin believed that it was necessary, both politically and economically, and argued that it would keep the Bolsheviks in power and enable Russia to recover from seven years of war (the First World War and the Civil War). He described the new system as a mixed economy – it had some capitalist features and some socialist (in that elements of the economy were controlled by the government, but not controlled by the workers, as they would be under true Marxism). Under the NEP the Bolsheviks retained control of railways and heavy industry, which are described in Marxism as the "commanding heights of the economy".

In addition, where War Communism had encouraged peasants to produce less (because surpluses were confiscated), the NEP would, it was hoped, encourage them to produce more (since they would be able to keep or sell surpluses), and within about eighteen months of the NEP being introduced, a small class of entrepreneurs did start to emerge: the NEPmen. At the same time, the kulaks – a class of wealthier farmers that had first emerged after Prime Minister Peter Stolypin's 1906 land reforms[24]– also benefitted from the NEP, and their numbers began to increase.

NEPmen at a busy Moscow market, 1923.

Many leading Bolsheviks such as Trotsky, objected on ideological grounds to the return, in any form, of capitalism (which brought with it private trade and profit) and the NEPmen in particular. According to historian Orlando Figes, "In 1921–22, literally tens of thousands of Bolshevik workers tore up their party cards in disgust with the NEP: they dubbed it the New Exploitation of the Proletariat."[25] Lenin responded by saying that the Bolsheviks had to take one step backwards in order to take two steps forward, "Let the peasants have their little bit of capitalism as long as we keep the power!"[26]

Effects of the NEP by 1924

- Grain production rose.
- Factory output increased.
- Average monthly wages doubled between 1921 and 1924.
- New socio-economic groups were created, such as the NEPmen.
- The Russian economy started to recover after the civil war.
- There was still no long-term solution to the question of land reform and the peasants.
- Industrial development remained limited and the manufacturing sector backward, compared with its Western counterparts.

	1913	1921	1922	1923	1924
Grain (million tons)	81.6	37.6	50.3	56.6	51.4
Pig iron (million tons)	4.2	0.1	0.2	0.3	0.75
Electricity (million Kwh)	1.9	0.5	0.8	1.1	1.5
Steel (million tons)	4.2	0.2	0.4	0.7	1.1
Cotton (million metres)	2582	105	349	691	963

Russian production figures, 1913–24

Conclusion

From the summer of 1921, Lenin was in increasingly poor health – he had survived an assassination attempt in 1918, and he had taken three further strokes – and by March 1923, he was paralysed on one side. As his health steadily declined, so did his influence over economic policy.

By the time of Lenin's death in January 1924, the NEP appeared to have been a success of sorts: the economy had been improving since 1921 (although key economic indicators for 1924 were still very poor compared with the same set of statistics for 1913).

On the surface, agriculture appeared to do better than industry under the NEP and it certainly

Lenin and his wife Nadezhda Krupskaya, 1922. The photo was taken during Lenin's recuperation from his first stroke.

offered the rural population infinitely more than War Communism had – namely the right to keep and sell surplus food (by 1924 the NEPmen controlled 75 per cent of Russia's trade) – but even by 1924 most problems associated with the peasants remained unsolved.

When Lenin died, the Communist Party was still divided between those who wanted to replace the NEP and those who wanted to maintain it – some party members, originally opposed to it had even became supporters of the programme. Nikolai Bukharin, for example, told gatherings of peasants "Enrich yourselves under the NEP!"[27]

CONSOLIDATE YOUR KNOWLEDGE

19. Give three factors for Lenin's introduction of the NEP Explain the importance of each factor.
20. How did Lenin justify the introduction of the NEP?
21. Outline two of the most important features of the NEP
22. How did Lenin encourage peasants to produce food under the NEP?
23. Who were the NEPmen and why were they important?
24. Why did some Bolshevik leaders oppose the NEP?
25. Why did Lenin maintain that the NEP was economically necessary?
26. Outline two important economic effects that the NEP had by 1924.
27. Explain the success of the NEP by 1924.
28. What economic problems had the NEP failed to solve by 1924?
29. Explain the main features of State Capitalism.
30. Explain the main features of War Communism.
31. Explain the main features of the New Economic Policy.

TASK

To what extent did Bolshevik economic policies lack consistency between 1917 and 1924? Use your own knowledge and research to explain the reasons why Bolshevik economic policies changed between 1917 and 1924.

2.4: The Success of Lenin's Economic Policies, 1917–24

By the time of Lenin's death in 1924, Bolshevik rule, along with the effects of the civil war, had altered the Russian economy almost beyond recognition. Three differing economic policies had been introduced, and historians generally disagree over whether or not Lenin achieved the economic aims he set himself in 1917. This section will look at Lenin's position in 1917, his economic aims at the time of the Revolution, and in the period immediately after it.

Lenin's economic aims and objectives

After the October Revolution, the Bolsheviks had won the support of some sections of the Russian working classes, in part through use of the slogan "Peace, Bread and Land". At that time, Lenin had believed in Marxist economic theory, where all means of production (such as farms, factories and other businesses) had to be controlled by the workers, in order to facilitate the creation of an egalitarian (socially and economically equal) society. Under a true Marxist society there would be a redistribution of wealth from bourgeois capital (middle-class owners and investors) to proletarian labour (working-class people who depended on employment for their incomes, and who owned little or no property).

However, the tough reality of trying to govern Russia caused Lenin to veer away from pure Marxism. In 1917 he realised that his economic aims had to change in order to cope with changing circumstances, and that he had to:

- Solve the problems of land ownership by dealing with the peasants.
- Increase agricultural production so that the population could be fed.
- Bring factory workers and manufacturing under the control of the state.
- Increase the productivity of factories.
- End Russia's involvement in the First World War, thereby reducing demand for war-related items and allowing the production of other goods.
- Create a socialist economy.
- Abolish capitalism and end private ownership
- Establish Bolshevik control of all economic areas, right across Russia.

In response to these new objectives, Lenin oversaw the introduction of three different economic policies – State Capitalism, (1917–18); War Communism, (1918–21); and the NEP, (1921–28) – that had varying levels of success [covered in section 2.3].

The bar charts below show the progress of key economic areas – grain production, coal production and factory output – under those three economic policies, from 1913–26. The lowest figures, from 1920–21, reflect economic output during the civil war and the worst years of War Communism, while under the NEP, from 1921 onwards, production recovered rapidly. However, the figures for 1924 are still noticeably lower than those for Tsarist Russia in 1913, a year before the start of the First World War.

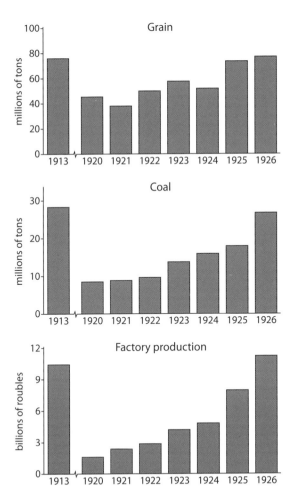

As Lenin said of the proletariat, during the 10th Congress of the All-Russian Communist Party in March 1921:

> never has its suffering been so great and acute as in this epoch of its dictatorship; and you all know it, having observed the life of your mates in the factories, railway depots, and workshops. Never before has the country been so weary and worn out.[28]

In April 1922, Joseph Stalin became general secretary of the Communist Party and continued to accrue political power thereafter. This had an effect on economic policy, among other things. For instance, Lenin had insisted on state control of overseas trade but Stalin was prepared to allow foreign companies to do business with Russia. Stalin and the ailing Lenin disagreed over the federal nature and even the name of the USSR, although they were able to reach a compromise.

CONSOLIDATE YOUR KNOWLEDGE

1. Describe the condition of the Russian economy in October 1917.
2. What opinion did Lenin and most Marxists have of the Russian economy before the Bolsheviks took power?
3. Why was it necessary for the Bolsheviks to bring the Russian economy fully under their control after the October Revolution?
4. What economic promises had Lenin made before October 1917?
5. Why did those promises create economic problems for Lenin after the October Revolution? Give two reasons.
6. Why did the civil war make it difficult for Lenin to achieve his economic aims after 1918?
7. Why were Russia's economic production levels in 1924 lower than those achieved in 1913?

How successful were Lenin's economic policies by January 1924?

- Lenin had tried to address the issue of land ownership but it was still causing a lot of economic problems.
- Lenin's attempts to bring the manufacturing sector and its labour force fully under state control had been partially successful.

- War Communism had actually led to a major fall in agricultural production but there had been a modest recovery under the NEP
- All large or important industries had been nationalised, and there had been some limited improvements to industry.
- Although Russia's involvement in the First World War had ended in March 1918, it had done a lot of economic damage. The civil war that immediately followed did further economic harm.
- Only a few elements of a socialist economy had actually been introduced by 1924.
- A very limited form of capitalism was restored under the NEP but the economy's 'commanding heights', such as heavy industry, remained in state control.
- The Bolshevik victory in the civil war enabled Lenin to take control of the economy, right across Russia.

CONSOLIDATE YOUR KNOWLEDGE

8. Name two of the economic aims Lenin had achieved by 1924.
9. Name two economic aims that he failed to achieve by 1924.
10. Which of the three economic policies was the most successful in your opinion? Give reasons for your answer.

TASK

Copy the table below and include examples of where, in your opinion, Lenin had either succeeded or failed in achieving his economic aims by 1924.
Add more rows as necessary.

Succeeded	Failed

2.5: Soviet society and culture, 1917–24

At the end of 1917, Lenin and his new Bolshevik government dreamed of a socialist society in Russia, with all aspects of life under Communist control and influence. This included the role of women and the family; the position of the Church; and popular culture and the arts in the new Communist state.

This section will examine the impact of Soviet culture on Russian society and look at some of the characteristics of that culture under Lenin between 1917 and 1924.

The role of women and the family

In their attempts to create a socialist utopia, the Bolsheviks alternated between an ideological approach to social policy and a pragmatic one, and ideology seems to have been the main influence on their attitudes towards women.

Until the First World War, Russia had been a conservative society in which the Orthodox Church had had a great deal of influence. Russian women therefore had few political rights, and society was dominated by men. For example, in Soviet Central Asia (which had been part of the tsarist Russian Empire), polygamy was often practised and women had even less influence. In their revolutionary zeal, some Bolsheviks had, in 1917, demanded an end to the traditional roles of women in nuclear and extended families. They introduced a series of measures which appeared to give Russian women certain freedoms for the first time.

In December 1917, family law was liberalised by a decree that challenged the institution of marriage. Divorce became much simpler and less expensive. Russia became the first country in the world in which both partners had the same rights to petition for divorce. By 1920, the country had the highest divorce rate in the world.

Notably, Lenin's government was also the first in the world to permit abortion. The Bolsheviks had long condoned the practice, and in November 1920 this was formally legalised when a decree was issued on the subject. From 1921 many state hospitals offered free abortions in an attempt to reduce the high number of deaths and medical complications caused by unlicensed terminations.

The Bolsheviks also greatly expanded communal living. Between 1917 and 1921, some large houses that had formerly belonged to members of the bourgeoisie or the aristocracy, were taken over and divided into flats for members of the proletariat. As economic circumstances began to improve, apartment blocks were built by the state for young families and single mothers.

There were also significant improvements to the rights and conditions of working women, particularly mothers. The government introduced paid maternity leave, and set up a government department for "the Protection of Mothers and Infants" that provided maternity clinics and crèches for women in the cities. The Bolsheviks' policies may have been based on Marxist ideology, but there were also practical reasons for drawing more women into the workforce: during the civil war there were extensive labour shortages. Women had already helped to fill gaps left by First-World-War casualties between 1914 and 1917: many men had been killed or injured during that time and, of those that survived, many were drafted into the Red Army. Women were able to fill the vacancies on production lines and on farms, and laws were introduced to give women equal rights in employment (including equal pay). The boost that female labour gave to both industry and agriculture was a factor that helped the Bolsheviks to win the civil war.

Women were also encouraged to take a more active role in politics and to join the Communist Party in the hope that they would play a full part in building a new, socialist society. In 1919, the Zhenotdel (the women's department of the Central Committee of the Communist Party) was established, led by figures such as Inessa Armand and Alexandra Kollontai.[29]

However, after the civil war, social attitudes towards women started to become conservative again, and, despite the Bolsheviks' attempts to end gender discrimination and stereotypes, the role of women had changed very little by 1924. Men had returned from service in the Red Army in 1921 and, as former soldiers returned to civilian employment, many women in the factories and the fields found that they were redundant. Some women found that the reform of divorce law had been a double-edged sword, as men could now walk away from their families and evade responsibility more easily than they had in tsarist times. Women had been encouraged to take an interest in political matters but they remained a minority, both within the wider membership of the party and, to an even greater extent, among its ruling elites.

CONSOLIDATE YOUR KNOWLEDGE

1. What was Lenin's attitude towards the role of women in society in 1917?
2. What steps did Lenin take to change the role of women after the October Revolution?
3. How did Bolshevik reforms in this area affect the traditional role of the family?
4. How did the Bolsheviks encourage women to seek employment?
5. How did the role of women change between 1921 and 1924?
6. Why is Alexandra Kollontai regarded by feminists as an important figure of the early Soviet era?
7. To what extent had the role of women really changed between 1917 and 1924?

GROUP ACTIVITY

As a group, research the impact of Bolshevik policies and changes to the role of women in Lenin's Russia. Think about:

- Women's role in the workforce.
- Women's position in the home.
- Women's position in the Party.
- Women's legal rights.

Discuss and present your findings.

Religion and the position of the Church

There were two main factors that influenced Bolshevik attitudes towards religion and the Russian Orthodox Church (an institution which had enjoyed a very powerful and prominent role in Russian society before the October Revolution of 1917). First, Marxists saw religion as an alternative ideology that could command the loyalty of an obedient populace. Therefore, it was a potential threat to the dominance of a Communist regime. Many Bolsheviks (including Lenin) were aggressively atheistic in their outlook. Second, the Russian Orthodox Church had been one of the pillars of tsarism. The Patriarchate – the office of the Church, which was run by bishops without interference from state government – had been re-established in 1917, and the power it and the Church wielded threatened the (still young) Communist state.

Lenin regarded the Church as an institution that not only sustained the "reactionary bourgeoisie", but would hinder social and economic reform of the entire country.[30] He believed that its influence had to be eradicated, and so the Bolsheviks began to encourage atheism in order to weaken the influence of organised religion across Russia.

Action against the Church began only a month after the Revolution. In December 1917, all educational institutions were placed under the control of the Commissar of Education, meaning there were to be no more Orthodox, Jewish or Muslim schools (or of any other denominations). Religious institutions lost any legal role in divorce and, from then on, only civil marriage procedures (those regularised by public officials) were recognised by the state.

The Decree on the Separation of Church and State was introduced in February 1918 to serve as a piece of catch-all "constitutional" legislation, against which the actions of religious groups and the state's regulation of religion could be measured. The decree banned all religious ceremonies and icons on public property; all religious education teachers were dismissed; and a government commissariat and special agency were set up to ensure that religion would not be promoted in schools, but that Bolshevik-approved philosophy could be. From then on, teachers had to be ideologically sound, in the opinion of the Bolsheviks. Freedom of religion was guaranteed on paper but, in reality, the only religion that people were completely free to practice was some form of Bolshevism.

Before 1917, the Orthodox Church had held a privileged position within wider Russian society but also in relation to the state. Under the Bolshevik regime, it was stripped of all its privileges. Religious groups were to be treated, in most respects, as other voluntary organisations had been. They were not allowed to make payments (such as tithes, taxes, weekly collections or membership fees) compulsory or impose punishments on their members.

Religious groups were also prohibited from owning land, buildings and other items, such as religious paraphernalia (which, in a religion as ritual-heavy as Orthodoxy, included a lot of silverware and works of art). In theory, if not always in practice, anything religious groups had owned was transferred to the ownership of the state and could be used with the permission of the local (Communist) authorities.

The government effectively made it illegal for bishops and archbishops to operate. The hierarchy (or high-level governmental structure) of the various

Churches began to fall apart. Some congregations exploited their new freedom from interfering bishops. The Bolsheviks, in turn, exploited divisions between the laity and parish priests, on the one side, and bishops, on the other.

In theory, religious material could still be produced and disseminated.[31] However, in practice, the Churches were prevented from printing books, pamphlets, magazines and newspapers, within months of the October Revolution. Many religious publishers, diocesan offices and so on had their printing equipment seized, while anti-clerical propaganda – such as leaflets, posters, newspaper cartoons, mock religious ceremonies in public places and polemical stage plays – was used to attack religious beliefs and institutions.

During the civil war, priests were seen as supporters of the White movement, but were usually no more than sympathisers. As a result, Red Army soldiers (often following the orders of local commanders rather than explicit instructions from the Kremlin) killed large numbers of priests. In the space of only six months, between the summer of 1918 and the early months of 1919, 19 bishops and over 100 priests were murdered in western and central Russia. More were killed in the same period, in outlying areas. On the fringes of the former Russian Empire, Bolsheviks sometimes meted out harsh treatment to clergy of all denominations (such as Lutheranism and Catholicism). Some historians have estimated that, between 1918 and 1924, more than 4,000 clergymen and more than 3,500 nuns were murdered. Most of those killings were carried out during the civil war and they reduced the power of the Church.

Many church buildings and monasteries were taken by the Reds and converted into local government offices, community centres, libraries, museums and so on. Sometimes, an especially inappropriate or humiliating new purpose (such as an exhibition on the evils of religion) was chosen for the building. Such acts reminded the populace that the Church was irrelevant and that faith should be placed in 'Leninist Marxism'.

From 1922, Trotsky was given the task of overseeing the Bolsheviks' anti-religion campaign. Famine-relief missions, which had managed to raise a lot of money for churches, were closed down and their assets seized. First, the Bolsheviks hoped that it would look as if the clergy no longer cared about the suffering of the masses. Second, the disappearance of the Church's famine-relief organisation created a pretext for seizing even more valuables from churches. Bolsheviks claimed that proceeds from the sale of church silver, icons, paintings, ornate furniture and so on (the sort of items which they had repeatedly ridiculed and sometimes destroyed in an attempt to weaken the hold of organised religion over the people) would be used to feed the starving.

Instead, the regime promoted non-religious (or even firmly Marxist) alternatives to long-standing Russian social conventions or institutions. Traditional marriage ceremonies were replaced by Red weddings, which were simple community gatherings in which stirring Communist music was sometimes played and local Communist officials could give 'rousing' political speeches in place of priests' sermons. Similar addresses were also a feature of many Red funerals – a drastic change from the elaborate rites of the Orthodox Church.

The Bolsheviks had evidently forgotten the warnings of Marxist theorist Friedrich Engels (repeated by Lenin himself in 1909) in which he cautioned against "a vociferous proclamation of war on religion".[32] The party had created substitutes for religious institutions, disrupted church services, broke down the organisational structure of the Church at local and national level, destroyed church property, murdered large numbers of clergymen and used the education system to show the young that religion was harmful. The regime had expected that traditional organised religion, faced with such hostile actions would soon die out.

By 1924, the Orthodox Church still survived – religious influences still remained in the private, domestic life of ordinary Russians – but the Church's position had been severely damaged: it had lost political influence and its profile within society.

CONSOLIDATE YOUR KNOWLEDGE

8. Give two reasons for Bolshevik opposition of the Russian Orthodox Church in 1917.

9. Why did Lenin want to promote atheism?

10. Account for the importance of the Decree on the Separation of Church and State.

11. In what ways did the decree affect organised religion?

12. Why did the Bolsheviks support attacks on the Church and its property?

13. What did the Bolsheviks hope to achieve through their use of anti-clericalist propaganda?

14. How did the status and influence of the Russian Orthodox Church (and organised religion in general) change between 1917 and 1924?

Popular culture and the arts

The Bolsheviks were keen to convert as many people to Communism as possible and Lenin believed that an important way to do this was through popular culture and the arts. He felt that the minds of the people could be infused with revolutionary ideas through art, propaganda, education and architecture.

The Arts

The Bolsheviks wanted to assume control (in the name of the proletariat) of the education system, literature, music and all other forms of cultural expression, and in the months following the October Revolution, the Proletkult (the Proletarian Culture organisation) was key to this approach, although it was a voluntary-sector organisation and not an institution of the Bolshevik state. It had been founded before the October Revolution, though some notable Bolsheviks (including Lenin's wife Nadezhda Krupskaya) were prominent members, and it felt that a political revolution must be followed by a cultural one and that art should be used to promote political and social messages.

Many Bolsheviks felt that they had to take charge of any cultural revolution in order to secure the long-term survival of the regime. They argued that culture was every bit as important as the political, social and economic change that Lenin sought to achieve.

Another important source of Russian cultural development was the government department Narkompros – which translates as either the Commissariat for Education or the Commissariat for Enlightenment. It was responsible for both culture and education. One of its stated purposes was to encourage and support artists of all kinds in Russia, including non-Communists, so long as those artists – known as 'fellow travellers' – were broadly sympathetic to "the ideals of the Revolution".

Indeed, in the early years of the Bolshevik state, the Commissariat aided the Proletkult: requisitioning many buildings – including some large, prominent ones in Moscow and Petrograd – for Proletkult use, and giving the group significant funding (tens of millions of rubles). For a few years after the Bolsheviks came to power, Proletkult had more influence over cultural activities than the numerous, and often weak, public bodies in the field of education and culture. By the early 1920s, about 80,000 people had joined this federation of cultural societies.

The overriding artistic style of this time came from the Constructivist movement, which in the first few years of Communist rule, dominated sculpture, graphic design and architecture. It is generally accepted that Constructivism was first observed in the work of Alexander Rodchenko and

Vladimir Tatlin who believed that art had to be 'built'. Constructivist artists focused on the characteristics of materials, and the sizes and proportions of pieces, initially through producing three-dimensional works with a somewhat industrial feel, but the term was soon applied to two-dimensional works such as posters and paintings. The movement had its origins in Futurism, where it was believed that technology was not only a tool with which a new society could be created, it was something which could inspire art itself; something to be celebrated in its own right. That belief inspired two important recurring messages in poster art: 'modern man' and 'the power of the machine'. With the blessing of the commissariat, Constructivism was influential in areas of Soviet art during the early years of the Bolshevik regime.

Propaganda and culture

Bolshevik propaganda came to dominate popular culture and the arts. The most heavily used medium was poster design – it was the least subtle way in which to ensure the masses would understand the party's message – but propaganda influenced a variety of different media, such as literature, drama, cinema, painting, sculpture, industrial design and architecture. Through these, Lenin aimed to create a fantasy world, in which he had already brought about the perfect socialist society. The Bolshevik leadership expected ordinary Russians to believe that such a society actually existed, despite the reality of everyday life around them.

The Bolsheviks used propaganda constantly throughout Lenin's leadership, in an effort to shape an entire political system and an entire society. And while propaganda was not a device unique to the Bolsheviks – it had existed across the world for centuries – using it to effect long-term cultural and political change (as opposed to a short-term change of attitudes in wartime, or a change in attitudes towards a particular product or company) was unusual. Bolshevik efforts also differed from most Western governments and their public-relations work in at least two other respects: first, their aims were unusually ambitious due to the scale of social and economic problems in Russia; and second, the Bolsheviks were fighting a civil war between 1918 and 1921.

In May 1919, at the height of the civil war, Gosizdat (the State Publishing House) was founded. In theory, all book and periodical publishing, except that already controlled by public bodies, was placed under its control. In practice, and for a number of reasons – such as the existence of other publicly-owned publishers (principally academic institutions and Moscow's city council), and Gosizdat's difficulty in obtaining supplies of paper – there were ways in which authors and editors could continue to publish without the input of the State Publishing House.

However, with the vast bulk of the population being illiterate, the Bolsheviks were quick to appreciate the potential of new types of visual media, such as radio and cinema and Russian radio engineers were keeping pace with developments in the Western world. For instance, by 1922, Moscow could boast of having the most powerful radio station in the world. So few Russian people owned radio sets, however, that it was necessary to install loudspeakers on some streets and in some important buildings. Likewise, films were used to imprint the Bolshevik message firmly on the minds of the masses. The works of Sergei Eisenstein – he later directed *Battleship Potemkin* (1925) and *October* (1928) – were noteworthy, particularly because of the new film techniques he used.

Traditional visual media were also used, like the theatre. Following a decree in August 1919, all theatres in Russia were nationalised and publicly-performed drama was controlled by the government thereafter. Bolsheviks hoped that it could help to win over audiences to their cause.

Then, in 1920, along with the formation of the Department of Agitation and Propaganda, came the term 'agitprop'. Applied to extremely politicised (and usually simplistic or exaggerated) art, agitprop could be expressed through a number of different media (such as pamphlets, works of fiction and short films). It too was applied to the theatre: using large numbers of performers, agitprop companies sometimes delighted audiences with lavish, open-air epics. Predictably, these included dramatised re-enactments of the October Revolution, and one such large-scale production was staged in Petrograd, on the Revolution's third anniversary.

Agit-prop was backed by:

- Lenin's efforts to push up literacy rates.
- The reintroduction of stringent official censorship of newspapers.
- Networks of trained and uniformed 'agitators' in rural areas.
- Groups of agitprop theatrical performers, some of whom toured Russia on special agitprop trains.

By 1924, the Communist Party under Lenin had taken control of all sources of opinion and information. The Bolshevik message was being relayed through the press and posters, and through painting, sculpture and literature and all other forms of media.

Agitprop trains were frequently used during the civil war. Here fat capitalists command a blindfolded White soldier to fight against the Bolshevik Red Army.

Education and young people

Lenin realised that there was no point in trying to introduce peasants to literature if they couldn't read. The elimination of rural illiteracy became a priority and education began to play an important role. The party aimed to create successive generations of young people who would be completely loyal to the Communist regime, and its 1919 programme described schools as "an instrument for the Communist transformation of society".[33] Under the new regime, even learning the alphabet could carry a political message:

A = All power to the soviets

B = Bolsheviks

C = Communists

Between 1914 and 1920 the percentage of children of school age who actually attended school fell from over 90 per cent to under 25 per cent. Literacy rates were slightly lower in 1917 than they had been twenty years earlier, and they fell again between 1917 and 1921. The civil war made it impossible for the Bolsheviks to impose their will on the whole country and reduced the amount of money available for schools and education.

As discussed, religious education teachers were dismissed from all state-funded schools in February 1918 (under The Decree on the Separation of Church and State), and all teachers were expected to conform with Bolshevik ideas. Leninist-Marxist thought began to influence what was actually taught in schools, which was to have profound effects on the Soviet education system. The Bolsheviks believed in all-round education, without any vocational specialisation. Traditional subjects were dispensed with in favour of independent activity and controlled learning based on themes such as nature, labour and society.

On 1 October 1918, a law establishing 'uniform labour schools' came into effect, wherein every school was to be known by that title along with its district and a number. Schools were brought under the control of the Commissariat for Education, who obeyed the orders of the new regime. Teachers and pupils were forced to conform with Bolshevik ideology. Standard systems of elementary education (for pupils aged 8–13) and secondary education (for pupils aged 14–17) were imposed on all of Russia, along with a standard, modern curriculum. Attendance at school was made compulsory and schools became co-educational. In the early years of the new regime, new theories of education were adopted and new teaching methods tried with mixed results.

In December 1919, the Sovnarkom issued a decree on literacy. The new policy was called 'the liquidation of illiteracy'. In the early 1920s, the decline in literacy was halted and even reversed. By the mid-1920s, the Soviet government claimed that half the population over primary-school age and two thirds of men could read, and by 1924, after efforts were made to eradicate any remaining illiteracy among urban factory workers and skilled tradesmen, the regime claimed to have made great progress in education.

	In 1914	In 1924
Total number of schools	101,917	85,662
Total number of pupils	7,030.254	6,527,739

However, much of the progress in the battle against illiteracy was not made by the state education system at all but by the Communist Party and its subsidiary bodies – namely the Komsomol (The Communist Union of Youth). This social-cultural organisation was set up by the party in October 1918 and was initially aimed at young people aged 14–28. It offered its members leisure activities, sports, drama clubs and so on, but it also had a focus on education. The Komsomol set up 'reading rooms' in cities, towns and large villages, where peasants could take advantage of classes for adults. Newspapers, pamphlets and some books were freely available (though these had already been censored, and many were published by the party itself).

In 1922, came the formation of the Young Pioneers: children aged 9–14 could join this group, then apply to join Komsomol (and at the age of 23, a Komsomol member could then apply for membership of the Communist Party). Komsomol undertook various tasks on behalf of the party, such as publicly denouncing enemies of the regime and (in later years) providing volunteer labour for public construction projects. Over time, the ideological element of the youth group became stronger and there was more of an emphasis on preparing young people for military service. By 1925, Komsomol had about 1.7 million members (about 5 per cent of those Soviet young people eligible to join the group).

Architecture

The communist values of the new state were also expressed through architecture. Architects and planners drew up grandiose schemes for remodelling cities, including Petrograd, but so great would the cost of implementing even parts of these plans have been that none were ever taken seriously by the Bolshevik regime. The more avant-garde architects argued that buildings for revolutionaries should be made from revolutionary materials (by which they meant iron, glass and concrete).

Perhaps the most extreme example of this new type of Soviet architecture is provided by the 'Monument to the Third International' (also known as 'Tatlin's Tower'), which was designed by Vladimir Tatlin, but never built. It was intended to house the headquarters of the Comintern (the Third International). Tatlin was a member of the Constructivist artistic movement, which believed that art should serve a social or political purpose; and he was a Futurist, which advocated modernisation and cultural rejuvenation [see p.97]. These new ideas also influenced Soviet architecture under Lenin.

Conclusions

- As a result of Revolutionary idealism, many new cultural forms and ideas had developed by 1924.
- A large number of talented artists left Russia between 1917 and 1924, and most never returned.
- The Bolsheviks used various cultural media in their efforts to indoctrinate the Russian people. The value of cinema and radio in that regard has been recognised.

CONSOLIDATE YOUR KNOWLEDGE

15. What was the role of the Commissariat for Education?

16. What was the Proletkult?

17. Why did some Bolsheviks resent the attention and funding that the Proletkult received?

18. What different methods did the Bolsheviks use to promote their cultural values?

19. Briefly describe the features of agitprop

20. Explain two of the important changes that the Bolsheviks introduced within the education system.

21. What were the two main Communist youth organisations? What was the role of each?

22. Outline the aims of the Constructivist movement in Russia between 1917 and 1924.

23. What were the aims of the Futurists?

24. Explain the importance of cinema and radio within Russia between 1917 and 1924.

TASK

Research the different aspects of Soviet society
and culture under Lenin. Think about:

- The role of the arts
- The role of the media
- The role of education
- The role of youth organisations

Discuss and present your findings.

Revision Section: 1917–24

This section will give a summary of the main events and developments in Russia under Lenin, and the creation of the world's first Communist state, from the October Revolution in 1917 to Lenin's death in January 1924 – a period heavily concerned with the regime's political and economic survival.

Students need to appreciate the impact that such events had, in that period, on both the Bolshevik government and ordinary Russians, so there will be a brief synopsis of key events and some sample exam questions. This will help to consolidate knowledge of key events of the period and explain their importance for the Russian government and the people. This should make it easier to prepare for formal assessment-unit tasks and other assignments.

Independent research, looking at the key figures and events, will also help to develop a better understanding of Lenin's Russia; in particular, why the Bolsheviks won the civil war. Lenin's economic policies, the effects of those policies and the types of culture promoted by the Bolshevik state must also be fully considered.

Turning point 1: The Russian Civil War, 1918–21

It is essential to examine both the causes and effects of the civil war. Although the Bolshevik victory removed most effective opposition to the regime, the civil war also created a number of additional problems for Lenin and his comrades.

Causes of the civil war
- Bolshevik Russia was weak, militarily.
- Russia was also isolated, diplomatically.
- There was a wide ideological gulf between the Red (Bolshevik) and White (conservative, liberal, socialist and so on) sides.
- Russia's allies in the First World War (Britain, France and so on) had a strong fear of Communism; were hostile to the new regime; and hoped that Russia would stay in/re-enter the war.
- Therefore, those allies actively assisted the Whites.
- The Treaty of Brest-Litovsk was unpopular, even within the Bolsheviks.
- The Whites and their foreign allies posed a military threat to the existence of the Bolshevik state.

- In addition, some political opposition to the Bolsheviks remained within Russia (such as that from the Left SRs).
- Lenin welcomed the prospect of a civil war.
- Trotsky organised and led the Red Army.

Effects of the civil war

- Foreign intervention had no significant military effect.
- White forces were defeated.
- Political opposition to the Bolsheviks was effectively eliminated within Russia.
- The Bolsheviks scored a great propaganda victory.
- Lenin and Trotsky were shown to be competent and dynamic leaders.
- The Red Army was forged into a highly effective fighting force.
- The Bolshevik government was able to extend its control over (almost) all of Russia.
- The Bolsheviks used economic policies to hold on to political power.
- The Bolsheviks completed their consolidation of power.
- Many civilians were killed.
- There was damage to infrastructure, industry and the agricultural sector.

Turning point 2: War Communism, 1918–21

It is important to understand the aims, features and effects of War Communism; Lenin's need to introduce it; and the successes and failures of this economic programme.

Aims of War Communism

- To keep Lenin in power.
- To win the civil war.
- To ensure that the Bolshevik regime would not collapse.
- To defeat the Whites and push their foreign allies out of Russia.
- To bring the economy under the full control of the state.
- To feed and supply the Red Army and industrial workers.
- To replace State Capitalism, the previous economic programme, as it had failed to meet the needs of the new Bolshevik state.
- To better fit in with Lenin's ideology.
- To end any vestiges of capitalism.
- To control the means of production.

Successes of War Communism
- Contributed to the Bolshevik victory.
- Meant that the Red Army was better supplied than the Whites were.
- Allowed the Bolsheviks to extend their control over various aspects of life.
- Helped to keep Lenin and Trotsky in power.
- Helped to defeat the Whites and their foreign allies.

Failures of War Communism
- Led to famine and many deaths.
- Repressed the peasants ruthlessly.
- Failed to halt the decline in agricultural and industrial production.
- Increased opposition to the Bolsheviks led to uprisings against them.
- Brought Russia to the brink of economic collapse.
- Created a lot of resentment (particularly because of Red Terror and the seizure of surplus food).

Turning point 3: The NEP, 1921–24

The New Economic Policy replaced War Communism. Like the two economic policies which preceded it (War Communism and State Capitalism), the NEP was intended to be temporary. The main aim was to allow Russia to recover from seven years of war (between 1914 and 1921).

Aims of the NEP
- To allow the economy to recover.
- To implement the change necessary after the failures of War Communism.
- To reconcile the masses with the Communist state.
- To restore the profit motive and thereby boost agricultural production.
- To improve food production.
- To encourage a recovery within the manufacturing sector.
- To relax economic policies and state control.
- To replace food seizures with taxation in kind.
- To keep the Bolsheviks in power.

Successes of the NEP
- Russia's economy recovered between 1921 and 1924.
- Agricultural production increased.

- Industrial production increased.
- There were no more significant anti-Bolshevik uprisings, between 1921 and 1924.
- The Russian economy became more stable.
- Large numbers of workers remained under state control.

Failures of the NEP

- It led to divisions within the Communist Party.
- Some Bolsheviks (such as Trotsky) were opposed to its capitalist elements on ideological grounds.
- The peasant problem had not been fully resolved.
- The emergence of NEPmen increased resentment in other sections of the population.
- There was no proper restructuring or modernisation of agriculture or industry and no increase in efficiency.

PRACTICE EXAMINATION QUESTIONS, 1917–24

Based on format of questions for CCEA Unit AS2, Option 5 (Russia).

These questions are for individual or class-based use and study. Questions from past papers and specimen papers can be accessed through the CCEA GCE History microsite:

www.rewardinglearning.org.uk/microsites/history/gce/past_papers/index.asp

These are some sample 8-mark and 22-mark examination-type questions, which will help students to prepare and practice for assessment tasks for this period.

8-mark questions (short responses)

a) Explain how Lenin helped the Bolsheviks to win the Russian Civil War.
b) Explain how Trotsky helped the Bolsheviks win the Civil War by 1921.
c) Explain why the Whites lost the civil war by 1921.
d) Explain the main features of War Communism.
e) Explain the reasons why Lenin introduced the NEP
f) Explain the cultural features of Russia during Lenin's leadership

22-mark questions (essay answers)

- "Without Trotsky's leadership, the Bolsheviks would not have won the civil war in Russia." To what extent do you agree with this verdict?

- "The Bolsheviks were politically united but the Whites suffered from political divisions, which is why they lost the civil war by 1921." How far would you accept that judgement?

- "Bolshevik economic aims and methods lacked consistency between 1918 and 1924." How far would you accept this statement?

- "In the period between 1917 and 1924, the NEP was the only successful economic policy of Russia's Bolshevik government." How far would you accept this verdict?

- How far would you agree that the advancement of women was the most important cultural effect in Russia between 1917 and 1924?

Endnotes

1   Figures taken from Lynch, Michael, *Reaction and Revolution: Russia 1894–1924*, eBook (4th ed., Hachette, 2015), p.120

2   It was thought that, within weeks, Britain and France could expect a surge of German troops on the Western Front and a huge offensive.

3   Lenin, V.I. and Gregory Zinoviev, *Socialism and War*, eBook (1915)

4   Trotsky, Leon, *My Life: An Attempt at an Autobiography*, eBook (1930)

5   Lynch, *Reaction and Revolution*, eBook

6   However, Lenin believed that any territorial losses would be temporary, and to a certain degree, he was correct. By 1941 the USSR had regained almost all of the territory it had given up in 1918.

7   Known in full as the Workers' and Peasants' Red Army.

8   Lenin in a telegram sent 23 August 1921. *From* Sebestyen, Victor, *Lenin the Dictator* (Hachette, 2017) p.396

9   Lenin, V.I., 'A Contribution to the History of the Question of the Dictatorship', 20 October 1920, www.marxists.org/archive/lenin/works/1920/oct/20.htm

10 Trotsky speaking to the Petrograd Soviet, 4 June 1918. *From* Figes, Orlando, *Revolutionary Russia, 1891–1991: A History*, eBook. (Metropolitan, 2014)

11 For most countries in this era, that would have been considered normal army practice but it, along with an officer corps and a rank structure, had long been rejected by many Bolsheviks (especially those associated with the less-effective Bolshevik forces that had existed before the creation of the Red Army).

12 Between February and June 1918, the Red Army was an all-volunteer force and propaganda was important in encouraging men (and party members and unskilled urban workers in particular) to enlist to defend the revolution.

13 Service, Robert, *A History of Modern Russia from Nicholas II to Vladimir Putin* (Harvard University Press, 2005) p.105

14 After the delaying tactics employed by the Russian delegates during armistice negotiations, Berlin had grown suspicious of the Bolshevik government.

15 Service, Robert, *The Russian Revolution, 1900–1927*, eBook (Macmillan, 2009)

16 Kolchak was a Russian naval officer who was persuaded to return to Russia by the British government, but who passed most military responsibilities on to other generals. He once governed an area of roughly 300,000 km^2 with 7 million inhabitants.

17 A legion of volunteer armed forces composed predominantly of Czechs (with a small number of Slovaks) who fought with the Allies during the First World War.

18 Figes, Orlando, *A People's Tragedy: Russian Revolution, 1891–1924,* (Jonathan Cape, 1996) p.560

19 Lenin, V.I., 'Draft Decree on Workers' Control', *Pravda,* 3 November 1914

20 Lenin in 'Immediate Tasks of the Soviet Government', March–April 1918. *From* Smith, S.A., *Russia in Revolution 1890–1928,* (Oxford University Press, 2017), p.221

21 Service, Robert, *Lenin: A Biography* (Pan Macmillan, 2000), p.352

22 Phillips, Steve, *Lenin and the Russian Revolution* (Heinemann, 2000), p.56

23 Lynch, Michael, *Reaction and Revolution: Russia 1894–1924*, eBook. (4th ed., Hachette, 2005)

24 Following the 1905 revolution, Peter Stolypin was appointed as prime minister. He introduced a series of land reforms with the aim of preventing political radicalisation of the mainly conservative peasantry. By the time of his assassination in 1911, his reforms had been fairly successful and a new class of land-owning peasants – the kulaks – had been created.

25 Figes, *A People's Tragedy*, p.771

26 From Oxley, Peter, *Russia, 1855–1991: From Tsars to Commissars* (Oxford University Press, 2001) p.6

27 From Lynch, Michael, *From Autocracy to Communism: Russia 1894–1941*, eBook (Hodder, 2008) p.162

28 Lenin, V.I., *Collected Works, Volume 32*, eBook (Lawrence & Wishart, 1965)

29 Kollontai was the first woman to be a member of any European government. She wrote books and articles that promoted free love and greater sexual freedom for women. Such ideas shocked most Russians, outraged some high-ranking Bolsheviks and led to a reduced political influence after 1921.

30 Service, *Lenin: A Biography*, p.442

31 It was not until the end of the 1920s that Stalin would ban such activities outright.

32 Lenin, V.I, *Collected Works, Volume 15*, eBook (Lawrence & Wishart, 1963)

33 Corin, Chris and Terry Fiehn, *Communist Russia Under Lenin and Stalin* (Hodder Education, 2002) p.284

STALIN'S RISE
TO POWER 1924–41

This chapter will examine:

3.1: The reasons for Stalin's rise to power, such as his strengths compared with the weaknesses of his political opponents during the power struggle.

3.2: The significance of Lenin's Testament, the importance of Stalin's position as general secretary, and the limitations of Stalin's opponents during the power struggle.

3.3: The relative importance of the various factors that formed the basis of Stalin's political power, such as the use of terror, propaganda and the personality cult.

3.4: Stalin's use of terror – in particular, the purges between 1934 and 1939.

At the end of this chapter there will be a summary of the causes and effects of some of the key events in this period, along with some exam-style questions.

3.1: Stalin's Rise to Power, 1922–29

Stalin's key dates and events, 1922–29

1922	April	Stalin elected General Secretary of the Communist Party.
1922	December	Stalin helps to establish the USSR.
1924	January	Lenin dies. Stalin supervises funeral arrangements.
	May	The Central Committee suppresses 'Lenin's Testament', at Stalin's behest.
1925	January	Trotsky forced to resign as war commissar.
	December	At 14th Communist Party Congress, Stalin puts forward the idea of Socialism in One Country.[1]
1926	January	Stalin publishes his work on ideology, *Concerning Questions of Leninism*.
1928	October	The first of the Five-Year Plans for the economy is published. Stalin attacks the 'Right' faction of the party, which favours the NEP
1929	January	Trotsky is expelled from the USSR and goes into exile, initially to Turkey.
	April	The first Five-Year Plan is approved by the Party Congress.

Stalin's early years, 1879–1912

Between 1924 and 1941, Joseph Stalin – born Josef Dzhughashvili – wielded considerable political power. As historian John Laver explains, "Stalin was one of the few individuals who made history, rather than just being part of it."[2] But for such a prominent figure, very little is known about his childhood since, during his time as a dictator, he destroyed a lot of sources of information about the early part of his life. Until recently, for instance, historians believed he was born in Tiflis, Georgia on 9 December 1879, but recent evidence suggests that he was actually born a full year earlier than he claimed – in 1878.

When Stalin was fifteen, he won a scholarship to the Orthodox seminary in Tiflis (now Tbilisi) and spent five years there training to be a priest. However, he began to turn his attention to politics and he slowly lost his religious faith. His involvement in extremist politics increased until, in May 1899, he was expelled from the seminary. In 1926, he described his induction into the world of political agitation, "I became an apprentice in the art of revolution".[3]

Between 1899 and 1903, he began to put his thoughts about revolution on paper. He absorbed the works of Lenin, and those of other anarchist and revolutionary socialist writers. In 1903, Stalin was arrested by the Okhrana (tsarist secret police) and sentenced to internal exile in Siberia. During the 1905 Revolution he was in the Caucasus, but in December of that year, at the RSDLP congress in Poland, he met Lenin for the first time. Lenin was impressed by the organisational ability and dedication that Stalin had displayed.

Between 1907 and 1912, Stalin spent several years in internal exile or in prison. Such experiences helped to shape his character and political outlook. In 1912, he started signing his articles and pamphlets with the pseudonym 'K Stalin' – 'Stalin' supposedly meant 'man of steel', just as 'Lenin' meant 'man of Lena'. He had used many other aliases before that and been known by nicknames, such as 'Koba'.

Stalin as a young man. From his secret police file.

The emergence of a revolutionary, 1912–17

In 1912, Lenin nominated Stalin for a position on the Communist Party's central committee. Stalin didn't attend the meeting, and his nomination was opposed by other members of the committee – most other Bolsheviks were middle-class Russians who focussed on the intellectual battle that lay ahead, while Stalin was a working-class Georgian who was ready for a physical fight – but Lenin co-opted him anyway and asked him to write a long article for Bolshevik newspapers on the nationalities issue.

For Stalin most of the period between 1912 and 1917 was spent in further periods of internal exile and spells in prison: he was arrested by the Okhrana at least eight times in the years leading up to 1917.

In March 1917, after the February Revolution, Stalin was the first high-ranking Bolshevik to reach Petrograd. In fact, until Lenin returned in April, Stalin was the de facto leader of Bolsheviks within Russia, despite being a relative unknown outside the party. He had attended the odd conference in Western Europe but, unlike most leading Bolsheviks, had never lived abroad for any length of time.

In the aftermath of the July Days, Lenin and other senior Bolsheviks had either fled Russia or, like Trotsky, been arrested. Stalin now temporarily resumed the role of leader on the ground. His profile was increasing for a number of reasons – for instance he had become editor of *Pravda* – and when elections to the central committee were held, only Lenin and Gregory Zinoviev [see p.211] received more party member votes than he did.

At a committee meeting in October 1917, Lenin revealed his plans to seize power. Some leading Bolsheviks – including Zinoviev and Kamenev – opposed Lenin on this, but Stalin pledged his full support. And while his true role in the October Revolution is still unclear, during those "ten days that shook the world", his position in the party was undeniably important.[4]

The growth of Stalin's political power, 1917–22

In October 1917, after the successful seizure of power, Stalin was rewarded for his hard work and his loyalty to Lenin and made commissar for nationalities. In addition, he was one of only seven members of the Politburo – the Communist Party's inner cabinet. In November 1917 a new core group, the All-Russian Central Executive Committee, was set up and authorised by the Central Committee to decide "all emergency questions".[5] It consisted of just four men: Yakov Sverdlov, Lenin, Trotsky and Stalin.

The new government faced many political threats, particularly between 1918 and 1921 [see p.54], but the party was also experiencing internal conflict – namely frequent clashes between Stalin and Trotsky. Stalin did not trust the former Menshevik, and greatly opposed Trotsky's decision to use former tsarist army officers in the Red Army. This marked the start of a very bitter and very personal conflict between the two men. Trotsky later criticised Stalin for gaining too much political power "with the aid of an impersonal machine" (the party bureaucracy Stalin had created).[6] In an effort to reduce bickering between the pair, Lenin even recalled Stalin to Moscow for a short while.

Stalin's focus during the civil war was the 'nationalities question': most of the nations within the former Russian Empire wanted independence and Stalin strongly opposed this. He was especially keen to keep Armenia and his native Georgia under Russian control. He adopted a policy of centralisation and, by 1921, had crushed most separatist movements (although the Baltic states and Finland had gained their independence several years before). But most Bolshevik leaders – including Lenin, who could be incredibly ruthless – were shocked by some of the methods Stalin used to suppress the threat of these different nationalities. Stalin had been involved with the Cheka right from the inception of the force and he fully supported using them during the Red Terror. The merciless secret-police organisation sought and destroyed any 'counter-revolutionary' threats, whether real or anticipated [see p.60].

By December 1922, the nationalities question had been resolved through a combination of repression, and through the establishment of the USSR – the Union of Soviet Socialist Republics. Stalin had suggested the name, but the idea came from Lenin. Non-Russian nations on the fringes of Russia were now to be given a degree of autonomy (at least, as much as any group can have in a one-party dictatorship), as opposed to Stalin's suggestion to fully incorporate the other nations into Russia – by force if necessary.

Stalin increases control of the party, 1919–22

One of the ways in which Stalin spread his influence most easily was by using his drive, energy and administrative ability to manage the internal structures of the Communist Party. Since the Revolution, he had been strengthening the party's bureaucracy and building a powerbase, making himself all but indispensable. In April 1919, Lenin appointed Stalin as the head of the People's Commissariat of State Control, which, in February 1920, became the People's Commissariat for Workers' and Peasants' Inspection (Rabkrin). Stalin was now in control of state bureaucracy, including the civil service and the police force, until April 1922.

At the heart of the Communist Party were four important committees or sub-groups – the Central Committee, the Secretariat, the Politburo and the Orgburo – and each of these had an important role within the Bolshevik dictatorship.

- **Central Committee** – the supervisory body.
- **Secretariat** – the executive arm of the Central Committee, responsible for overall management of the party.
- **Politburo** – the department of the Secretariat responsible for the formation of policy, with a working group at its head.
- **Orgburo** – the department of the Secretariat responsible mainly for party structures and personnel management, also with a working group at its head.

As Lenin clarified in 1919, "The Orgburo allocates resources and the Politburo decides policy."[7]

By 1922, only Stalin was a member of all four party bodies. He was already a member of the Orgburo and Politburo, and acted as the liaison officer between them, and through the Orgburo he had direct control over membership issues and the party's organisation throughout Russia. Then, in April 1922, Lenin appointed Stalin as the first general secretary of the Communist Party (head of the Secretariat) in a move that historian Orlando Figes describes as, "arguably the worst mistake in the Revolution's history."[8]

Stalin certainly exploited this new position as general secretary [see p.120] – he had already created a very effective, locally-based, party machine and, as head of the Secretariat, which was responsible for party membership, he now had an enormous power of patronage. The Secretariat held a personal file on every single member, and if Stalin doubted the loyalty of any local official – loyalty to both the party and to him – that person could be (and swiftly was) replaced with someone more 'reliable'.

Despite the lucrative position he held, Stalin's political opponents – such as Trotsky, Zinoviev and Kamenev – failed to act against him until it was too late. But while their complacency was their weakness – Trotsky once described Stalin as "the party's most eminent mediocrity"[9] – Stalin's low-key approach was his strength. All his rivals in the power struggle underestimated the political threat he posed. He was also helped by Lenin's ban on party factionalism (introduced in March 1921), which limited debate within the Bolsheviks and made senior members afraid to criticise Stalin in case they were seen as disloyal to Lenin and to the party itself.

Finally, from 1922 onwards, Stalin benefitted from Lenin's worsening health. Lenin's 'Testament' [see p.123] suggests that he might have acted to stop to Stalin's empire-building within the party, had he been physically strong enough to do so. Instead, when he died, Stalin's path to total domination was clear.

CONSOLIDATE YOUR KNOWLEDGE

1. Explain the significance of Stalin's role between the February Revolution and the October Revolution.
2. Why was Stalin's post as commissar of nationalities important?
3. Give two reasons for the strength of Stalin's position within the party in 1917.
4. Give two reasons for the political rivalry between Stalin and Trotsky between 1917 and 1924.
5. Why had some Bolshevik leaders criticised Stalin for his actions in the period between 1918 and 1921?
6. Outline the advantages Stalin possessed in April 1922 when he was appointed general secretary of the party.
7. What were the weaknesses of Stalin's political opponents between October 1917 and 1922?

TASK

Create a timeline that outlines Stalin's political career between 1914 and 1924.

3.2: Stalin and the Power Struggle, 1922–29

The power struggle between Stalin and his political rivals may seem to have followed Lenin's death, but in reality it had started a few years earlier. This section will examine Stalin's success, which came as a result of three main phases – his time with Lenin (1921–24); his defeat of Trotsky and the 'Left' of the party (1924–27); and his defeat of the 'Right' of the party (1927–29).

Stalin and Lenin, 1921–24

During this period, several factors helped Stalin improve his chances of becoming leader and lessen the chances of his rivals (such as Trotsky and Kamenev) but perhaps the most crucial was his appointment to general secretary in April 1922. From then until Lenin's death in January 1924, Stalin continued to strengthen his power base within the party.

Before he became general secretary, Stalin had already held a number of important roles within both the Party and public bodies, but his new post gave him effective control over the Orgburo and, through it, decisions about personnel and organisational structures. From one end of Russia to the other, he appointed his supporters to key local and regional posts within the party, and he could rely on those supporters to be loyal to him, personally. Through this system of patronage, they helped him exercise an increasing degree of influence over the central components of the party machine (for example within party congresses). Stalin also benefitted from Lenin's banning of factionalism in 1921 – when Lenin curbed party opposition to the NEP [see p.81]. Groups within the party found it almost impossible to dissent from any policy, or to criticise the leadership, without it looking as if they were questioning Lenin's word. That situation was of great benefit to Stalin as it made it easy for him to silence most of his opponents.

Between 1923 and 1925, under what was termed the 'Lenin Enrolment', came a significant expansion of the Communist Party in both membership figures and geographical reach. The number of party members almost doubled, from 340,000 in 1922, to 600,000 in 1925 but, most significantly, most of the new recruits had been drawn from the proletariat (working classes). They were therefore more likely to identify with Stalin, whose hard work had allowed him to rise through the ranks, than with his arch-rival, Trotsky, a middle-class intellectual who could often seem unpredictable and untrustworthy (at least, these were the perceptions that Stalin tried to cultivate).

Trotsky at a party meeting, 1923.

Naturally, Stalin manipulated and exploited the opinions that party members had of him and of his rivals. By the time of Lenin's death, support for Stalin at a grass-roots level within the party had increased quite a lot and, even at that stage, he had (more or less) outmanoeuvred Trotsky. Stalin had played the part of a loyal follower of Lenin, and claimed to be suspicious of Trotsky – a former Menshevik who had joined the Bolsheviks only three months or so before the October Revolution.

Other Bolsheviks shared Stalin's apparent misgivings. Trotsky may have demonstrated considerable skill as an administrator and a military strategist during the civil war, but he could also be very arrogant and slightly aloof. Members were also wary of his Jewish background (for centuries Russia had been a deeply anti-Semitic society) and he had neglected to build up support within the party. He may have had admirers of his own, but he had failed to build a power base strong enough to withstand Stalin's machinations. He had greatly underestimated the level of control that Stalin had over the party machine, and the influence he had built up by 1924.

Finally, Stalin would benefit from Lenin's declining health. Lenin had taken his first serious stroke in May 1922. He had recovered fairly well by October, but he had a second stroke on 15 December. The Bolshevik Party was very hierarchical and, with Lenin busy recuperating, there was virtually no one to keep Stalin in check. He was effectively free to do as he pleased within the departments of the party that, as general secretary, he now controlled and so he appointed more and more of his supporters to key positions throughout the party. Furthermore, Stalin used his position as general secretary to take charge of Lenin's doctors and restrict his visitors – essentially controlling who could and couldn't see him. Confined to his wheelchair and with his doctors imposing a restriction that "Vladimir Rich may dictate every day for 5 to 10 minutes", Lenin was effectively Stalin's prisoner.[10] When Lenin had a third stroke in March 1923, he did not really recover. He entered into a period of terminal decline and died on 21 January 1924.

CONSOLIDATE YOUR KNOWLEDGE

1. How did the use of patronage help Stalin build a power base within the party between 1922 and 1924?

2. In what way did Lenin's ban on factionalism within the party help Stalin?

3. Explain the significance of the 'Lenin Enrolment' in Stalin's rise to power.

4. Give two reasons for Trotsky's unpopularity within the party, relative to Stalin.

5. How was Stalin helped by the state of Lenin's health, particularly after 1922?

The defeat of Trotsky and the 'Left' of the party, 1924–27

When Trotsky heard of Lenin's death, he was on his way to a spa town in Georgia. He arrived twenty-four hours too late for Lenin's funeral. Stalin, on the other hand, had organised the funeral and was able to play the part of chief mourner. He arranged for Lenin's body to be embalmed and placed on display in Red Square, Moscow – even though Lenin and his wife had been strongly opposed to the idea – and used his prominence at the funeral as a way to imply that he was Lenin's natural successor.

Certainly Stalin enjoyed strong support from the party's rank and file, as well as the local leaders that he had placed throughout the Communist Party – as historian E.H. Carr put it, by January 1924 "the elite party of Lenin was becoming the mass party of Stalin"[11] – but two main threats to Stalin's position remained:

1. Lenin's Testament.
2. His political rivals, such as Trotsky and Bukharin.

Lenin's Testament

For the last fourteen months of his life, Lenin was effectively in semi-retirement, and from December 1922 to January 1923 he wrote his 'Testament' – a series of recommendations about the future of Russia and the party, almost analogous to a will. In the document, Lenin discussed Stalin's unsuitability for high office, warning that Stalin was rude and selfish, and therefore unsuitable for the role of party secretary.[12]

> Comrade Stalin, having become Secretary-General, has unlimited authority concentrated in his hands, and I am not sure whether he will always be capable of using that authority with sufficient caution … Stalin is too rude and this defect, although quite tolerable in our midst and in dealing among us Communists, becomes intolerable in a Secretary-General. That is why I suggest that the comrades think about a way of removing Stalin from that post.[13]

Stalin was not, however, the only one to come in for some criticism, several other prominent members of the Central Committee were scrutinised too. Bukharin was supposedly a little too dogmatic and unable to defend Marxist principles in a robust debate – but was also described as one of "the most outstanding figures (of the youngest ones)" and capable of development[14] – while Zinoviev and Kamenev clearly still hadn't been completely forgiven for having opposed the October Revolution during the planning stage.

Lenin had intended for his Testament to be published after his death – it also ought to have been read to delegates at the party's 12th Congress in 1923 – but it contained so many criticisms of the leading Bolsheviks that, in May 1924, the Central Committee agreed to its suppression. Stalin ultimately benefited more than anyone else from this decision, as Lenin appeared to favour passing the leadership to Trotsky, but even he came in for some criticism – "[Trotsky] is personally perhaps the most capable man on the Central Committee, but he has displayed excessive self-assurance"[15] – and in the end, Lenin's wishes regarding the appointment of his successor were not clear. Taking advantage of that uncertainty, Stalin presented himself as Lenin's true heir.

Lenin's legacy and Trotsky

By 1922, due to Lenin's poor health since 1921, a *troika* (triumvirate) had emerged to govern Russia. It was intended to be a temporary measure, and consisted of three key figures:

1. Lev Kamenev: Shortly before the Revolution Kamenev had spent some time in internal exile with Stalin. However, he was also Trotsky's brother-in-law.
2. Gregory Zinoviev: Trotsky had shown him up in the past and so Zinoviev disliked him more than he disliked Stalin.
3. Joseph Stalin.

Until about 1920, Kamenev had got on well with his brother-in-law (later, he and Zinoviev would became Trotsky's allies), so the extent to which members of the triumvirate disliked Trotsky may have varied. But Stalin's hated of Trotsky was deep and lasting – although that may not have been apparent to everyone in 1922 – and by 1924 their common dislike of Trotsky was enough to bind them together and isolate him from political power.

The three men feared Trotsky, and began a whisper campaign against him, dubbing him "a political Bonaparte" [16] – implying that, if he were to succeed Lenin, Trotsky would be as dictatorial and reckless as Napoleon. They accused him of threatening party unity and of being 'anti-Leninist', which, given the surge of Leninism that followed the party leader's death, was particularly damaging. As Zinoviev declared at Lenin's funeral, "Lenin is dead. Leninism lives!"[17]

Meanwhile, even in the early part of 1924, Stalin was giving lectures on 'The Foundations of Leninism'; and five days after Lenin's death, Petrograd was renamed Leningrad – Stalin was creating a godlike figure. He was keen to promote 'Lenin's legacy' – which in later years became an altogether more developed Stalin-led personality cult [see p.134] – since, in promoting this 'cult of Lenin', Stalin was able to make himself look like a loyal follower, friend and true heir of Lenin. He was also able to make Trotsky look like a disloyal troublemaker and a critic of Lenin.

So by 1924, Trotsky had become an isolated and unpopular figure with the party, and during the 13th Communist Party Congress in May that year, he faced heckling from Stalin's loyal supporters (who had increased in numbers thanks to the Lenin Enrolment [see p.120]). They were going to make sure that Trotsky had no opportunity to criticise 'Comrade General Secretary', but the War Commissar's tone was not antagonistic. Trotsky tried to reach out to his opponents and demonstrate his loyalty:

> None of us desires or is able to dispute the will of the Party. Clearly, the Party is always right … The English have a saying, 'My country, right or wrong', whether it is in the right or in the wrong, [the Communist Party] is my country.[18]

That October, Trotsky was his usual, outspoken self. To tie in with the seventh anniversary of the October Revolution, he published a long essay about the events surrounding it. Entitled 'The Lessons of October', it was as critical of the roles Kamenev and Zinoviev had played as Lenin had been.[19]

With this attack on the men of the triumvirate, it is perhaps no surprise that the campaign to undermine Trotsky intensified after 1924; and in January 1925, with his reputation within the party damaged, he gave up the post of war commissar. He held several less prestigious ministerial posts during 1926 and 1927, but was removed from the Central Committee in October 1927 (along with Zinoviev). A month later, he was expelled from the party altogether, and soon his role in organising the Revolution of 1917 would be erased from the Soviet version of history under Stalin.

Socialism in One Country and defeat of the Left

Accusing Trotsky of factionalism during the (fairly one-sided) power struggle, helped Stalin to eliminate the political threat that his main rival posed. Then, in 1925, Stalin started to isolate the other two members of the triumvirate, Zinoviev and Kamenev.

Zinoviev (the chairman of the Comintern) was chairman of the Leningrad Soviet, Kamenev was chairman of the Moscow Soviet, and they shared two major concerns. Firstly, persistent economic and social problems in Russia's two largest cities had not been properly addressed by the government of the USSR, and secondly, Stalin's hunger for power seemed to be increasing steadily.

By 1924, three years after its introduction, Communist Party members were still divided by the NEP Trotsky had always opposed the NEP, and he maintained his belief in "Permanent Revolution"[20] – a continuing struggle to establish Communist governments across the world – while Stalin realised that the USSR's economy had to be modernised. His response was the policy of 'Socialism in One Country', under which the government of the USSR would concentrate on building its own industrial economy and aim to make the country self-sufficient [see p.165]. Most people believed that Stalin's policy meant the continuation of the NEP

Kamenev and Zinoviev were both against Socialism in One Country. They and their supporters formed 'The New Opposition' and, at the 14th Communist Party Congress in December 1925, attacked the policy and the NEP However, Stalin's increased influence within the party meant that all their motions were easily defeated, and this led to a public rift between the three men. In 1926, Kamenev and Zinoviev (and their supporters in The New Opposition) joined Trotsky under the banner 'The United Opposition'. Within the Communist Party, they and their supporters (or those that were critical of Socialism in One Country) were referred to as the Left. Those, such as Bukharin, who supported Stalin's policy were known as the Right.

The United Opposition tried to present its ideas to the Central Committee in the summer and autumn of 1926 but Stalin or his allies were in control of every piece of the party's machinery – Stalin had increased the members of the Politburo from six to nine and the three new appointees were all his supporters[21] – and proposals from the Left stood no chance of being adopted.

By 1926, the Left and its three leaders – Trotsky, Zinoviev and Kamenev – had been discredited and removed from major positions within the party, which was now being controlled by Stalin and Bukharin (the most prominent figure on the Right). That year the policy of Socialism in One Country was officially adopted.

Zinoviev had been targeted first: as a former member of the triumvirate, he knew a lot about Stalin and was therefore seen as an immediate threat. At the Central Committee meeting in July 1926, he lost his seat on the Politburo. His Comintern post was abolished too. In December 1927, during the 15th Communist Party Congress, he was expelled from the party.

Trotsky was removed from the Central Committee in October 1927 and, like Zinoviev, was expelled from the party that November.

Kamenev was removed from the Central Committee in October 1927, and in December, he tried to address the Party Congress, expressing the hope that an accommodation could be reached between the Left and the rest of the party. He had no success: very shortly after that, he was expelled from the party, along with many other supporters of the Left. The views of the United Opposition were declared incompatible with those of the party itself.

Realising that the situation was now hopeless, Kamenev and Zinoviev gave in: they publicly severed their links with Trotsky and admitted that the Left had been in error. Their party membership was restored, but by 1932 they had been expelled again. In 1928, Trotsky was in internal exile in Central Asia, and in February 1929 he was expelled from the USSR, and the threat from the Left had been thoroughly defeated.[22]

CONSOLIDATE YOUR KNOWLEDGE

6. The triumvirate consisted of which three men?
7. Following Lenin's death, what was the triumvirate's political role?
8. Why was the part that Stalin played at Lenin's funeral politically important?
9. What were the two main political problems Stalin faced immediately after Lenin's death?
10. Why did the Communist Party decide not to publish Lenin's Testament?
11. Why was the failure to publish Lenin's Testament politically important for Stalin?
12. Briefly describe the Lenin cult created by Stalin.
13. Why did Trotsky become more unpopular within the party, during 1924 and 1925?
14. In what ways did Stalin display loyalty to Lenin?
15. What was Socialism in One Country?
16. Who opposed Socialism in One Country and why?
17. Why did Stalin take action against Zinoviev and Kamenev?
18. What were the main aims of the United Opposition?
19. What happened to the leaders of the United Opposition in 1927?

The defeat of the 'Right' of the party, 1927–29

Bukharin, and other figures on the Right of the party, had helped Stalin by attacking the United Opposition, and the process of expelling a large number of their rank-and-file supporters from the Party was under way, but with the Left having been defeated and removed from power, Stalin now turned on his erstwhile allies.

The NEP and the Right Opposition

Bukharin was a reasonably popular figure within the party, despite having been a supporter of the Left in the early days of the Bolshevik regime (notably at the time of the signing of the Treaty of Brest-Litovsk). He had moved to the Right and had become quite enthusiastic after the introduction of the NEP Stalin saw Bukharin as a potential political rival and he used the debate over the future of the NEP to damage his reputation.

The Left of the party had wanted to replace the NEP, while the Right had defended it, but in 1928 Stalin used his supporters to demand that the NEP (which Bukharin backed) be brought to an end so that he could introduce his own economic policies [see p.164]. Stalin wanted the state to develop an industrial economy for the USSR within a few years, and his view was that only Socialism in One Country could achieve that objective.

The Right Opposition defended the NEP, it also criticised the party's bureaucracy and Stalin's proposal that a new economic plan should be drawn up every five years. At Central Committee meetings during 1928, Bukharin expressed mild dissatisfaction with some aspects of Stalin's proposals, as did his allies on the Right – Alexei Rykov, the chairman of the Central Committee; and Mikhail Tomsky, the chairman of the Council of Trade Unions. Despite the opposition Stalin launched the first of his Five-Year Plans in October 1928 [see p.181], and began to make his move against his former Right allies.

The end of the Right Opposition

In 1929, leaders of the Right Opposition were publicly named and removed from all positions of power. Both Bukharin and Tomsky were removed from the Politburo that year and Bukharin declared, "Stalin will strangle us. He is an unprincipled intriguer, who subordinates everything to his lust for power."[23] By the end of 1929, the Moscow branch of the party had been purged of Right Opposition supporters and in 1930, Rykov was removed from the Politburo. The Right had been defeated.

Stalin was now the only one of the main 1917 Bolshevik leaders left in political power – he had skilfully outmanoeuvred his opponents and exploited the limitations of his rivals. As Bukharinput it, "Stalin knows only one means: vengeance and putting a knife into your back at the same time."[24] Historian Martin McCauley summed up Stalin's strategy, "He was a very skilful politician who had a superb grasp of tactics, could predict behaviour extremely well and had an unerring eye for personal weaknesses."[25]

Stalin had neutralised all threats to his leadership from within the party and now no one could challenge his decisions. He had created a dictatorship

CONSOLIDATE YOUR KNOWLEDGE

20. Outline the aims of the leaders of the Right Opposition.
21. Why was Bukharin opposed to the idea of Five-Year Plans?
22. What had happened to most Right Opposition leaders by 1929?
23. Why did Stalin take action against Right Opposition leaders?
24. What mistakes did the leaders of the Right make between 1928 and 1929?
25. Why was Stalin successful in the power struggle by 1929?

TASK

Create a timeline that outlines Stalin's political career between 1924 and 1929.

GROUP ACTIVITY

Using your own knowledge and research, explain why Stalin had won the power struggle in the USSR by 1929.
Discuss and present your findings.

3.3: Stalin in Power: Propaganda and the Personality Cult

Between 1929 and 1941, Stalin used various methods to retain power in the Soviet Union – terror, propaganda and the cult of personality. This section will look at the roles of these three main factors.

Emergence of terror

Stalin had already made use of state terror. In the 1920s, tens of thousands of counter-revolutionaries were labelled "anti-Bolsheviks", "bourgeois nationalists" or "deviationists" and imprisoned by the party acting on his orders. Then, between 1927 and 1929, during Stalin's somewhat one-sided battles against his Communist Party rivals (and especially during his campaign against the United Opposition), his opponents had begun to feel the presence of the secret police – called the OGPU since 1922.[26] However, those tactics were mild compared with those used in the early 1930s. No opposition was tolerated and Stalin's government used fear as a means of control over the people. Citizens were wary of party officials and dreaded the secret police.

Between 1929 and 1934, Stalin implemented collectivisation. He felt that the only way forward in agriculture was for each village to voluntarily unite their farms into one collective farm, allowing them to increase efficiency, afford machinery, and create a surplus that could be sent to the towns [see p.169]. Any resistance to collectivisation, or to his Five-Year Plan was crushed without mercy. Although some members of the Right had warned that collectivisation would (to put it mildly) fail to generate the desired results, Stalin and his dutiful supporters blamed failures to meet production targets on saboteurs and others who wished to undermine the government.

The 1932 'Riutin affair' was perhaps the last instance of genuine party opposition to Stalin. Right party member Martemyan Riutin had published a secret document in which he described Stalin as an "evil genius" and called for, amongst other things, an end to forced collectivisation.[27] Riutin and twenty-three of his followers were expelled from the party and were threatened with execution. Kirov spoke out against this and Riutin was sentenced to ten years in prison, before being shot in 1937.

The USSR had effectively become a totalitarian dictatorship by the early 1930s. Stalin supported an increase in the number of detention camps (there had been a few in the 1920s but the number of people detained was very small). So, following Politburo discussions in June 1929 and a Sovnarkom decree in July of that year, the 'Chief Administration of Corrective Labour Camps' – known by its Russian acronym, 'Gulag' – came into being in 1930. From that point, the number of camps was expanded rapidly and by 1934 there were approximately one million political prisoners in these corrective labour camps.[28] Some of those settlements were in very remote and inhospitable places (north of the Arctic Circle, for example) and later developed into industrial estates or towns [see also p.198]. In 1934, the Gulag system became part of the Commissariat for Internal Affairs (NKVD), as did the OGPU (secret police) and thereafter the secret police were known as the NKVD.

In 1933 and 1934, over one million members of the party (or roughly 35 per cent of the total) were expelled; the kulaks (property-owning peasants and thus the main victims of collectivisation) were eliminated as a class; and harsh measures were imposed on industrial workers too. In 1934, Stalin's government also conducted show trials for so-called 'wreckers': people who were blamed, whether likely or not, for every missed goal, broken machine or failure within the Five-Year Plans. Stalin accused former Mensheviks, and even a number of former high-ranking Communists (especially those 'Old Bolsheviks' who had been prominent before 1929), of being wreckers in these trials.

One of Stalin's Communist Party purge committees, 1 May 1933.

Terror had become an indispensable part of the Stalinist machine but far worse was to come in the great purges of the late 1930s. Lenin had been ruthless at times (had even planned purges of his own as early as 1921, though these were not implemented), but when Stalin embarked on his purges, they grew in scale until eventually his victims could be counted in the tens of millions [covered in section 3.4].

CONSOLIDATE YOUR KNOWLEDGE

1. How did Stalin deal with his political opponents between 1924 and 1929?
2. How did Stalin's approach to opposition figures differ between 1929 and 1934?
3. Why was the Gulag system expanded between 1930 and 1933?
4. How important was the Gulag system?
5. How did the Stalinist regime use terror to increase his power by 1934?

Propaganda

Bolsheviks had made use of propaganda since October 1917. The aim of Stalin's state indoctrination was to create a twisted version of reality in which the official view of things was normal (or at least unquestionable) and anyone who didn't accept it was an enemy of the state.

Stalin used propaganda on a massive scale to glorify the Soviet Union (and himself), and to tell the Russian people how much his government had achieved, especially in terms of economic development and productivity. Stalin used the same range of media that Communists had been using since the Revolution, namely newspapers, cinema, radio, graphic design, posters, poetry, drama and even fine art and architecture.

Among other things, propaganda was used for the following purposes:

- To inspire the people and gain their approval and assistance for government projects, such as the construction of power stations and factories, and the collectivisation of farms.

- To continually reinforce the message that Stalin was always right. Although this could cause confusion and intensify fear when people didn't understand what Stalin wanted, or when he issued two sets of orders that were incompatible.
- To make even mild or trivial forms of dissent against Stalin appear abnormal and harmful to society.
- To portray the USSR as a bastion of socialist virtue: a workers' republic threatened by the decadent and immoral capitalism and imperialism of the West.

Only the Soviet regime had easy access to broadcasting equipment and it controlled all forms of the media with strict censorship The two main state newspapers were *Pravda* and *Izvestia*, and their main role was to highlight the successes of Stalin's regime (both real and imaginary). Party institutions also controlled public celebrations such as May Day, the workers' holiday, and the anniversary of the October Revolution.

In the 1930s, the regime not only used propaganda to reshape views of contemporary events, it also attempted to rewrite history. The parts Lenin and Stalin played in the Bolshevik struggle and in government were exaggerated, making them more important and impressive. Every year, more books justifying Stalin's actions (and presenting him as the real hero of the Revolution and Lenin's closest follower) were published. Stalin even went to the lengths of having photographs and paintings from 1917–24 altered, to make his own image more prominent and to remove from history any trace of his former rivals, such as Trotsky.

CONSOLIDATE YOUR KNOWLEDGE

6. Why did Stalin use propaganda after 1929?
7. Describe the main features of Stalinist propaganda.
8. Why did Stalin and his government need to control all forms of the media?
9. Account for the importance of propaganda in the USSR of the 1930s.
10. In what ways was history rewritten by Stalin's regime?
11. Why did Stalin emphasise his links with Lenin?

TASK

Search online for examples of Stalinist propaganda that sought to rewrite history, and write a paragraph on the importance of Soviet propaganda posters and the role of the media under Stalin between 1929 and 1941.

The cult of personality

The personality cult arose between 1924 and 1933 during another period of political and economic change. Stalin needed the loyalty of the masses, and the appropriation of Russian culture was crucial. He could use the personality cult as a means of political control [covered in section 3.5].

The treatment of Stalin started to go beyond mere glorification of their leader. An early instance of the cult in action came in 1925 with the renaming of the city of Tsaritsin to 'Stalingrad', in honour of the USSR's new leader. Posters and statues of him were displayed in public buildings and almost on every street corner in the USSR. The media was already in the hands of the state, so almost every newspaper, book and film produced praised him, and he was given the credit for anything the country managed to achieve. On his fiftieth birthday in 1929, he received over three hundred and fifty greeting telegrams and cards from supporters and groups within the party. More than a few of the groups didn't exist. From 1929 onwards, extravagant parades were held every year on his birthday.

A number of posters were produced, showing him as a fatherlike figure, surrounded by adoring children. Schools did their 'civic duty' and helped ensure that pupils would grow up knowing just how brave and clever their great leader Stalin had been during the Bolshevik struggle for power, and how much he had done for the USSR since 1924. For the Russian people, he was being turned into a godlike figure, presented as alternative to religion – a 'faith' that Soviet citizens could celebrate openly.

The personality cult grew in scope and intensity from 1934 onwards and reached its peak during the great purges of the late 1930s. Stalin had become the embodiment of the USSR, and Communism had become Stalinism – a term first used in 1936 by Nikita Khrushchev who, at the time, was head of the party in the greater Moscow region. He had been very loyal to Stalin and had implemented the purges that killed about 90 per cent of his friends and colleagues.

No criticism of Stalin was permitted in any form, whether in public or private, and anyone who criticised their leader risked being reported to the NKVD (secret police). Instead, propaganda posters, films and articles tried to portray him as a man of the people, commonly known as 'Uncle Joe'. By 1939, loyal members of the party were spreading the slogan, "Stalin is the Lenin of today."[29]

By the mid-1930s, after almost twenty years of Communist rule, Russians had another tsar although, this time, he was a Bolshevik. The term 'Red Tsar' is one used by many historians.

CONSOLIDATE YOUR KNOWLEDGE

12. Why did Stalin's personality cult develop in the USSR?
13. What role did the mass media play in the cult?
14. What messages did the media deliver to the Russian people in order to portray Stalin as a great leader?
15. How did the personality cult intensify after 1934?
16. What were the political aims of the personality cult?
17. To what extent had Stalin become a Red Tsar by 1941?

GROUP ACTIVITY

Using your own knowledge and research, explain the role and importance of the personality cult as a means of control over the USSR between 1929 and 1941.
Discuss and present your findings.

3.4 Stalin and State Terror, 1934–41

In December 1934, Sergey Kirov, head of the party in Leningrad, was assassinated. He was a popular leader, and Stalin used his death to justify a significant expansion of the state-terror machine. This section will cover the three key aspects of Stalin's purges – the post-Kirov purges; the Great Purge; and their impact on the Soviet Union by 1941.

Kirov's death and the post-Kirov purges, 1934–36

On the afternoon of 1 December 1934, Kirov was shot dead inside the office building where he worked by Leonid Nikolaev, supposedly because Kirov had been having an affair with his wife. Stalin acted as chief mourner at Kirov's funeral – it was a huge propaganda opportunity that he certainly exploited – and became personally involved in the investigation. Nikolaev had been a minor official of the Communist Party before he had been expelled, and Stalin used this to launch large-scale purges within the party – issuing a decree authorising a swift and harsh response to "terrorist acts".[30]

Kirov's funeral procession, 6 December 1934. Stalin is on the right.

However many historians believe that Stalin had some role in Kirov's murder. Kirov was popular within the party and seen by some as Stalin's potential successor. He had been in charge of the party in Leningrad since 1926, and in 1930 became a member of the Politburo. He was an excellent public speaker and had been a loyal supporter of Stalin for some years.

In the early 1930s, when collectivisation was causing unrest, particularly in rural areas, the pace of economic change in the USSR had led to divisions within the party [see p.130]. Stalin demanded that the implementation of his plans proceed at full speed (even if there were social or economic problems as a consequence), but Kirov was concerned about the worsening living standards and working conditions of the proletariat. He wanted to slow down reforms.

The 17th Communist Party Congress was held in January 1934, and a majority of Party Congress delegates favoured Kirov's more moderate approach over Stalin's uncompromising stance. Stalin found it impossible to accept such a state of affairs. One theory, then, is that Stalin had grown jealous and suspicious of Kirov, who was younger and more popular within the party, had removed this potential political rival, and then used his death to justify the resultant purge.

Stalin had authorised some purges in Russia before 1934, but their scale had been limited; and in the early 1930s he had begun a process that, by the time it had finished, had created an apparatus of state terror on an industrial scale. Now he was quick to blame Kirov's murder on opposition elements within the party, led by Kamenev and Zinoviev, and also foreign agents. He used show trials and the purges to remove enemies of the state between 1934 and 1939.

In 1934 alone, over one million people (mainly from the Moscow and Leningrad areas) were arrested and executed. Prominent victims of the first wave of the post-Kirov purges included Kamenev and Zinoviev, who were also subject to these show trials. Defendants were often accused of having participated in one, or some, of the following crimes:

- Conspiracy with one or several foreign powers
- Conspiracy to overthrow or murder Stalin
- Conspiracy to restore capitalism
- Conspiracy to break up the USSR itself

The conspiracies were, of course, fictional. Many of the lower-ranking party members, who were executed because of some extremely vague or tenuous association with the Right, had joined the Communist Party some years earlier, under the Lenin Enrolment.

Stalin's orders were carried out by the NKVD (Commissariat for Internal Affairs) and, even today, those initials are infamous because of the role the NKVD played in the purges carried out between 1934 and 1939. From July 1934, the head of the NKVD (the commissar for Internal Affairs) was Genrikh Yagoda.[31] He had expensive tastes and spent large sums of NKVD money, occasionally on himself. In 1936, he too became a victim of the purges, but his corruption was only an excuse. There were more likely reasons for his demotion:

- He knew too much about Stalin's murderous activities and intentions.
- Crucially, he had stated, more than once, that there was no evidence to link Zinoviev with Trotsky.

He was demoted to the equivalent of postmaster-general in September 1936, stripped of privileges in January 1937, and sentenced to death in March 1938.

There was something of a lull in denouncements and executions, particularly during November and December 1936, which appears to have been connected with the adoption of the new Constitution of the USSR. It had promised many wonderful things: under Article 125, freedom of speech, of assembly and of the press was guaranteed. But, as Western critics of the USSR pointed out, a written constitution is worthless when supreme power is held by one political party or by one individual. In other words, the rule of law never existed in the USSR.

CONSOLIDATE YOUR KNOWLEDGE

1. Why might Stalin have regarded Kirov as a rival in 1934?
2. What orders did Stalin issue, just after Kirov's murder?
3. Who did Stalin immediately blame for Kirov's murder?
4. How did Stalin set about creating a 'terror state' between 1934 and 1936?
5. Why were Old Bolsheviks who had once held senior positions in the party executed? Of what were they accused?
6. What were the political effects of the post-Kirov purges by 1936?

The Great Purge, 1936–39

A noticeable characteristic of the Great Purge, the second wave of detentions and executions, was the increased use of show trials or perhaps the greater attention that the media gave to such spectacles. Defendants were condemned before members of the public, newsreel cameramen and newspaper correspondents (including many from other countries).

Some of those sentenced to death were formerly prominent figures within the party, but those affected can be divided into three main groups – namely the party; the armed forces; and the secret police.

The party

The war against the party began in earnest in 1936. The scale and intensity of operations was much greater than anything that had ever been seen before. The victims were what was left of the Left, Right or even 'Centre' factions. These were people who had ceased to have any real political influence ten years before but whose very existence was an embarrassment to Stalin. The labels 'Trotskyite' and 'Zinovievite' were applied to defendants, almost indiscriminately. For instance, Rykov and Bukharin were accused of being part of the 'Anti-Soviet Right-Trotskyist Block' yet they had consistently opposed Trotsky only a few months earlier, and Bukharin had even been a member of the constitutional commission that had drafted the new Soviet constitution of 1936. In fact, the description 'Right-Trotskyist' was a contradiction in terms.

After 1936, attention turned from political has-beens to current party members. The Secretariat [see p.118] issued secret briefings to regional branches of the party, giving details of fictional plots and many party members were accused of being Nazi agents. A lot of fear and hatred was stirred up by the 'Moscow Show Trials', which took place between 1936 and 1938. Party members made ludicrously unconvincing false confessions and even started hurling accusations at each other. They had been warned to be on the lookout for potential "spies, terrorist and diversion elements", and were expected to report to the NKVD any colleagues about whom they had the remotest suspicions.[32] Many eagerly made complaints about people against whom they bore grudges.

Many of the 'crimes' to which people confessed would have been impossible. Yet, in a directive issued by the Comintern in March 1938, Stalin claimed that the USSR was under threat from "a world conspiracy of reaction and fascism directed against the Land of Socialism".[33] It is believed that he observed most of the show trials in 1938 – the year in which Bukharin and Yagoda were tried.

Many party officials across the Soviet Republics were purged, accused of offences such as 'opposing the Five-Year Plans'. The party's rank and file was purged in order to remove supporters (and potential supporters) of any leaders who had already been removed, while minor policy disagreements and personality clashes were often the basis for purges at local level.

Ethnic nationalism in the non-Russian republics of the USSR was also seen as a threat and Stalin dealt with it in what was, by now, the usual fashion. At that time Nikita Khrushchev – Stalin's loyal supporter – was head of the party in the Ukraine and his brutality in the Ukrainian SSR was almost

legendary. In Georgia alone, two heads of the provincial government and four fifths of Communist Party administrators were purged.

Even Central Committee members and Party Congress delegates were not safe from the purges. In 1934, the Central Committee had 139 members but by 1939, only 41 remained; the 1934 Party Congress was attended by 1,966 delegates, but by 1939, only 798 of them remained. Of the 73 senior Communists who addressed the plenum (meeting of all members) of the Central Committee in February and March 1937, only 15 (Stalin and those close to him) survived until 1940 or later.

During 1937, the names of approximately 40,000 people appeared on the Politburo's execution lists and Stalin actually boasted of having signed the death warrants of many of his former supporters.

Stalin reputedly signing execution orders.

As historian Leonard Schapiro described it, the purges were "Stalin's victory over the party".[34] They were designed to ensure that:

- Any potential source of opposition to Stalin, as an individual, would be eliminated.
- Any resentment caused by collectivisation and industrialisation would not result in political opposition.
- Stalin would remain the supreme leader of the USSR and the party until his death.

- Those citizens who survived the purges would be too scared to say or do anything, even implicitly, that was critical of the regime.

The armed forces

By 1937, the military was the only state institution left that could stand up to Stalin, so he turned his attention to the Red Army and Soviet navy, both of which were badly affected by the Great Purge. Both services suffered but the effects on the Red Army were much more significant in the long run, its leadership all but destroyed. From May to June 1937, during the 'Trial of the Generals', eight leading Red Army generals were arrested, tried in secret before confessing to a range of crimes, and then shot dead. In addition, the purges resulted in the death of three out of the five marshals of the Soviet Union (senior Red Army officers, promoted to that position in October 1935), fourteen (of the sixteen) army commanders, and 37,000 other officers, many of them with years of experience. Similarly, by 1938, the Soviet navy had lost all of its Flag Officers (the pre-war Soviet equivalent of admiral of the fleet, to rear admiral).

By killing so many senior officers, Stalin had severely damaged the USSR's defensive capabilities, just as Europe was rearming and heading towards the Second World War. Most of the experienced officers arrested were accused of treason and executed. Their replacements lacked experience. In some cases, they were totally unsuitable for any military (or naval) post but were appointed anyway because they were loyal to Stalin, and by 1939 the Soviet armed forces were completely under Stalin's personal control.

The secret police

The NKVD played a major role in the implementation of the purges, yet even they were not safe. Yagoda had been head of the secret police since 1934, had been involved with the party since before the Revolution and had personal links with many of its members, but in 1936 he was removed from this position and replaced by Nikolai Yezhov.

Yezhov was a ruthless figure who would arrest and execute anyone, and everyone, that Stalin wanted to 'liquidate', without asking any questions. In his time as commissar for internal affairs during the Great Purge, he was witness to the execution of 3,000 of his own secret policemen, officers included, and oversaw the most intense phase of terror. From 1937–38 the NKVD recorded the executions of 681,692 victims who were executed in the prisons before even reaching the Gulags.[35]

In the summer of 1938, Yezhov, notorious for his role in the Moscow show trials, was forced to resign. He was tried and, in 1940, was executed. He was succeeded by Lavrentiy Beria, head of the Georgia branch of the party. Beria's name was actually on a list of officials that were to be purged, but he had been forewarned by the local NKVD chief, so he flew to Moscow and spoke to Stalin. The dictator agreed that Beria had been loyal for a long time and offered him Yezhov's job. Yezhov was thus transformed, almost instantly, from perpetrator to victim – proving that nobody within the Soviet Union was safe from Stalin, not even leaders of the secret police.

In November 1938, following a joint decree from the Sovnarkom and the Central Committee, Beria was instructed to scale down the level of arrests across the USSR, thereby stopping the NKVD's mass repression of citizens.

CONSOLIDATE YOUR KNOWLEDGE

7. Why were so many party members accused of being 'Trotskyites', during the Great Purge?
8. Why did Stalin organise show trials of Old Bolsheviks?
9. Why were so many officials purged from local and regional branches of the party?
10. Why were the armed forces purged from 1937 onwards?
11. What was the main effect of purges on the armed forces?
12. Why did Stalin purge the leaders of the secret police by 1938?

The impact of the purges by 1941

From 1934 to 1939 the purges affected millions of people across the Soviet Union. Victims were either killed or sent to the labour camps. Most of these came from social and political brackets that Stalin despised or feared, and were often accused of the following type of crimes:

- Supporting opposition groups
- Industrial sabotage and 'wrecking'
- Bribery
- Food hoarding

The NKVD were instrumental in the purges but they, in turn, were reliant on assistance from ordinary citizens. In the USSR of the late 1930s, people rushed to denounce their friends and neighbours. Informers were everywhere – in factories, offices, public places and communal apartments – and it has been estimated that, at the height of the purges, millions of citizens had become informers. Families were put under pressure to renounce arrested relatives, while people crossed the street to avoid 'enemies of the state'.

People were encouraged to act as informers through a variety of approaches, both incentivising and punitive. For instance, the property of someone who had been denounced could be confiscated by the NKVD and given to an informer as a reward. While on the other hand, those who had been arrested were put under pressure to give statements implicating friends, colleagues and neighbours in anti-Communist conspiracies, black-market activities or other crimes that the NKVD had invented. A favourite tactic of the secret police was to promise reduced sentences or immunity from prosecution, take the eagerly offered statement and then shoot the person who had given it anyway.

Millions of people disappeared as a result of the purges. The 1937 census of the Soviet Union showed that the population was significantly lower than expected. This presented Stalin with a serious problem – closer analysis of the findings would have revealed that millions of people had vanished and large numbers had died in suspicious circumstances. As a result he suppressed the report and imprisoned the 'incompetents' who had compiled it. Then, for a short time at least, NKVD activity directed at ordinary citizens was reduced.

It increased again between 1938 and 1939, and by then the Great Purge had resulted in the detention of one person for every eighteen in the population as a whole. By 1939, Stalin had eliminated any potential internal threat, but now Nazi Germany posed an external threat. This signalled the end of the Great Purge, but not the purges themselves, and between 1939 and 1941, they continued in particular geographical areas. In 1940, tens of thousands of people were forcibly removed from the three Baltic States after the Soviet conquest of the area, and dispatched to towns in Siberia. It is difficult for historians to produce accurate and reliable figures for the loss of life under, what has been called, the Great Terror, but historian John Laver has estimated that about 20 million people were arrested, 7 million of whom were executed.[36]

By 1941, the purges had badly damaged the party, the armed forces and the USSR itself. Stalin had used ruthless methods to create a totalitarian state – a Soviet dictatorship – and the citizens of the Soviet Union had paid a terrible price for that achievement. It was a price that Stalin seemed to dismiss, reputedly telling US ambassador Averill Harriman, "one death is a tragedy – a million deaths is a statistic."[37]

The historian Sheila Fitzpatrick described the Great Purge as being similar to the French Revolution: "It was state terror in which erstwhile revolutionary leaders were the most visible victims … In the Great Terror of the Russian Revolution, by contrast, only the chief terrorist, Stalin, survived unscathed."[38]

A French poster from 1939, showing many of the Old Bolsheviks and commentating on their fates.

CONSOLIDATE YOUR KNOWLEDGE

13. By 1939, how had the purges impacted on ordinary people in the USSR?
14. Describe the role of the secret police (NKVD) during the Great Purge.
15. What were the main political effects of the purges by 1941?
16. What were the social effects of the purges by 1941?
17. How did Stalin benefit politically from the purges by 1941?

3.5: Culture in Stalin's Russia, 1924–41

Culture played an important role in Stalin's Russia. As with propaganda and the personality cult, this meant the use of the arts and media as a means of control over the people of the USSR. This section will look at the use of the mass media and creative arts as channels through which political control was reinforced in three key areas: popular culture and the arts; culture and Soviet society; and religion and the position of the Church.

Popular culture and the arts

The Soviet Government had not established full control over the arts by 1924, despite the concerns of some senior Bolsheviks [covered in section 2.5]. That changed dramatically under Stalin and after 1924 the Soviet state came to control virtually everything in the cultural sphere.

Stalin imposed a 'cultural revolution' on the Russian people between 1928 and 1932 in which the regime tried to construct a new Soviet socialist culture, supposedly with the aim of obliterating all traces of the former 'bourgeois' one. To Stalin, this meant attacking bourgeois elements such as the intelligentsia, cultural elites and 'fellow travellers' [see p.96].

From 1933 onwards, the use of propaganda intensified and the personality cult grew stronger. It was primarily for those reasons that the state became much more heavily involved in the cultural arena. It hoped that propaganda would encourage a loyalty to Stalin among the citizens, and that they would then automatically support government policy.

Socialist realism

In January 1925, the Russian Association of Proletarian Writers (RAPP) was formed in order to ensure that writers promoted socialist values in their work – under what has been termed "the cult of the little man".[39] The RAPP endorsed poetry and prose (especially novels) that presented an idealised version of Russian workers – praising the achievements of those who were shaping a new society around the Five-Year Plans.

Suddenly, in April 1932, a decree was issued "on the Reconstruction of Literary-Artistic Organizations".[40] The RAPP and similar creative associations, including the Proletkult, were shut down, replaced by the Union of Soviet Writers, which was fully controlled by the state. In 1934, at the First Congress of the Union of Soviet Writers, Maxim Gorky – a founder of the socialist realism literary method – said that writers were "engineers of the soul".[41] Yet despite the poetic words, the truth was that the intellectuals and dreamers who had once steered artistic endeavours in the USSR had been swept aside and replaced with bureaucrats chosen by the Communist Party. From this point on, the only artistic style that the state endorsed was socialist realism, which used realistic imagery to present a glorified depiction of communist values and which was often noted for its huge scale. It marked the end of the cultural revolution – under socialist realism all works would reflect the achievements of the Communist regime and its great leader.

Almost all painters, sculptors and illustrators adopted socialist realism. Paintings and posters showed Soviet labourers and artisans in vast industrial facilities or pristine prairie landscapes that stretched to the horizon. In perfect harmony with each other and with their new equipment they toiled under the watchful eye of Lenin or Stalin for the same aim – the creation of the perfect society. It became the universal style among tutors at Soviet art schools – the most important of which was the Academy of Arts, which went by various names in the 1920s and 1930s. In 1934, painters and sculptors were informed that some subjects (religion, non-official political views) and certain 'decadent' styles or genres (expressionism, conceptualism and abstract art) were unacceptable to the state. By 1936, any artists who challenged Stalin's socialist realism were removed from their positions within education or elsewhere, before being sent to Gulag camps or executed.

Similarly, while some writers immersed themselves in socialist realism, many (such as Boris Pasternak, author of *Doctor Zhivago*) did not, and those who opposed the new policies were either purged or forced into exile. The works of some Russian literary giants (including Tolstoy) were also edited to fit the mould of socialist realism, and to promote Stalin's new Russian cultural nationalism, which, despite the odd piece of 'workers-of-the-world-unite' rhetoric in speeches and articles, had expunged any genuine internationalism from Russian Communism.

Those Soviet writers who remained were left with two main tasks: first, they were expected to detail the struggles of (hypothetical) working-class heroes; and second, relay the many triumphs of Stalin and the Communist Party (whether they were triumphs in reality or not). One frequently addressed subject was 'the defeat of the capitalist threat'. Their books were cheap and many libraries had been built, meaning this literature was readily available to tens of millions of Soviet citizens. By 1937 the overall adult literacy rate had risen to 75 per cent (from 56 per cent in 1926), although, as in earlier years, the male rate remained higher than the female rate.[42]

All forms of media, such as newspapers and magazines, used socialist realism in the form of graphic design and descriptive literature, to promote an idealised vision of life in the USSR. Like many of the plans drawn up for avant-garde buildings in the early 1920s, that vision was impressive enough, at first glance, to take in some Western writers with Communist sympathies but it was totally divorced from political reality.

No art form was safe from interference. Like its literary equivalent, the Russian Association of Proletarian Musicians (RAPM) had been abolished. Composers were also expected to do as they were told. For instance, the most widely acclaimed Russian composer of the time was Dmitri Shostakovich. His opera 'Lady Macbeth of the Mtsensk District' was first performed in 1934 and was popular with selected audiences for about eighteen months. One (officially approved) review said that it "could have been written only by a Soviet composer brought up in the best tradition of Soviet culture".[43] Then, out of the blue, a number of articles in *Pravda* appeared to criticise the work. In January 1936, it began a run at Moscow's Bolshoi Theatre, which Stalin and several Politburo members attended. The composer was worried. Two days later, *Pravda* published a critical review of the opera, and in response, he withdrew his next composition, the 'Fourth Symphony' from public. It has been suggested that he was responding to an official ban, and that this action likely saved his life. Shostakovich survived this threat but continued to have a complex and often difficult relationship with the Soviet government.

Socialist realism was also the only permissible style for the visual arts in the USSR. Film directors (and indeed, all artists) who utilised complex techniques were accused of 'formalism' – the use of techniques and forms accessible only to the elite, rather than simplified for the people – and were not, therefore, favoured by the regime. Even the world-renowned filmmaker Eisenstein [see p.98] tried to conform with socialist realism, but his attempts severely damaged his reputation and career.

Even architecture was not exempt: its equivalent of socialist realism was 'Soviet neo-classicism', which survived as the official, state-sanctioned style until after Stalin's death. The term, 'Stalinist architecture' is sometimes applied, especially to the grandiose and more extreme examples. A few office blocks in Moscow, Minsk and so on, were immense, and many statues – which were either of Lenin or Stalin, or paradigms of socialist virtue, such as the noble Soviet worker – were built on a massive scale. Such statues appeared in almost every settlement of note in the USSR, from large cities to medium-sized towns. They were probably the ultimate physical manifestation of Stalin's personality cult through this cultural revolution.

By 1941, as the cultural propaganda spread throughout towns and cities, there was an obvious difference between the images that bombarded the Russian people and the lives they actually led. The Communist Party had set out to create a new proletarian form of universal culture (as opposed to what they saw as the 'bourgeois' culture that had existed prior to the 1917 Revolution), but socialist realism was not promoting true socialist values and its portrayal of the USSR was distinctly unrealistic, both factually and politically. As Orlando Figes puts it, "The Stalinist regime abandoned its commitment to the creation of a proletarian culture".[44] Stalinist culture had been developed and used as just another means of control.

The role of the Komsomol

In 1926, the Komsomol [see p.100] formally became a Communist Party institution, meaning that, ultimately, it could be controlled by the Central Committee. In 1927, Komsomol had about 2 million members, all aged between fourteen and twenty-eight, but by 1940, there were 10 million.[45] They pledged loyalty to Stalin and the Communist Party.

During Stalin's cultural revolution, young Communists were encouraged to find and attack 'bourgeois' cultural elements. For example, Komsomol members would enthusiastically attack groups such as the 'fellow travellers', or disrupt a theatrical performance if the play's underlying message, subject matter or style had been judged to be incompatible with Stalinist cultural doctrines. Komsomol also helped to spread Communist propaganda and were encouraged to denounce enemies of the state.

In order to aid the implementation of the Five-Year Plans, Komsomol volunteers helped build new factories, power stations and about twenty 'Sotsgorods' (socialist cities closely linked to industry). A number of these new cities were created around existing towns in Siberia, east of the Ural Mountains.

When public events were held to celebrate Stalin's birthday or the May Day 'Workers' Holiday', Komsomol provided young flag bearers, cheerleaders and acrobats for large-scale displays across the Soviet Union.

CONSOLIDATE YOUR KNOWLEDGE

1. What were the aims of Stalin's cultural revolution between 1928 and 1932?
2. What was the role of the RAPP in Soviet culture under Stalin?

3. Explain the features of socialist realism under Stalin by 1941.
4. What were the main effects of socialist realism on Russian literature?
5. Explain how socialist realism was used as propaganda by Stalin by 1941.
6. How did the Komsomol deal with culture of which the regime did not approve?
7. How did Stalin use the arts and media as a means of control by 1941?

TASK

Copy out the table below and summarise the impact socialist realism had on the USSR by 1941 in the following areas.

Arts	Impact of socialist realism
Paintings	
Literature	
Media	
Music	
Architecture	

Culture and Soviet society

The role of education

Stalin realised that the educational reforms Lenin had introduced had achieved few of their political aims. There were fewer schools and pupils, in 1924, than there had been in 1913. Stalin decided that, in order to achieve his economic aims, the education system (and literacy rates in particular) would have to be improved drastically and so made formal education one of his top priorities. His regime would also use the education system to instil unquestioning obedience into the Soviet citizens of the future.

Stalin presented his education reforms as measures that would allow both his publicly stated vision (that of a Marxist paradise) and his actual aims to be realised. Through education he hoped to strengthen his position as dictator and allow him to strengthen the country economically and militarily.

Until 1935, schools were run at local level, but The Education Law of 1935 centralised control under the People's Commissariat for Education. The law also made a number of important changes to the system:

- All children now had to attend school for at least ten years (between the ages of five and fifteen).
- They had to follow a common curriculum and use only state-approved textbooks.
- Educational progress was to be checked by exams and tests, devised and overseen by the Commissariat for Education.
- Homework and uniforms became compulsory in all schools (uniform regulations even required girls to tie their hair in pigtails).

It was hoped that strictly regimented and highly efficient schools would produce a strictly regimented society and a highly efficient economy. Education would give people the knowledge and skills they needed to do all the jobs in the burgeoning Soviet economy.

By 1941, these reforms seemed to be working to a certain extent. Literacy rates were dramatically improved – in 1926 only 51 per cent of people over the age of ten could read, but by 1939 this had risen to 81.7 per cent – and, between 1929 and 1941, the total number of pupils in Soviet schools rose from approximately 12 million to 35 million.

Some pupils stayed on at school for an extra three years and left when they were eighteen, however, those pupils had to pay fees. It was that aspect of the system in particular that helped to create an elite group in Soviet society. By 1941, many of those who received more specialised training or education between the ages of sixteen and eighteen were the children of party bureaucrats or government officials. The party was dominating education, as it dominated everything else. For example, as early as 1932, roughly one third of university undergraduates had been nominated by the party.

At that time, the most important research institution was probably the Academy of Sciences. In fact, in 1925, the Soviet Government recognised it as such and the institution acquired a 'Soviet' prefix. In 1934, Stalin had it moved from Leningrad to Moscow, and regional branches were established to the east of the Urals. Many district centres were also later opened across the USSR. This body oversaw the research of more than 50,000 scholars – not all of whom were scientists, since other institutions had merged with it, particularly in the nineteenth century – and these academics were finding that, like artists, that they had to stay within limits imposed by Stalin's regime.

The role of women and the family

During Lenin's time as Russia's political leader, women had, in theory at least, been granted economic and political equality [see p.90]. Stalin too, despite his own social conservatism, did encourage women to work and was keen to push up female literacy rates – especially in rural areas. The female literacy rate for the USSR as a whole still lagged behind the male literacy rate by 1941.

Since the early 1920s, abortion and divorce had also been made readily available to most women, however this meant that, by the 1930s, the USSR had the highest divorce rate in Europe, with roughly half of marriages ending in that way. Stalin wanted to address this. The regime began to emphasise the importance of women as mothers and homemakers, calling for women to return to their 'traditional' roles. Seemingly this was an attempt to restore traditional family values, however the underlying reason was Stalin's belief that more social stability and a larger population were necessary for the economic development of the USSR. As such, a decree of 27 June 1936 outlawed abortion, except "in those cases where the continuation of pregnancy endangered life or threatened serious injury to the health of the pregnant woman".[46] This was designed to boost the birth rate to increase the Soviet population.

In 1930, the Zhenotdel – the women's department of the Central Committee of the Communist Party, established by Lenin in 1919 [see p.91] – had been officially dismantled. The party had declared that all the aims of the Zhenotdel had been achieved and that it was therefore unnecessary. Then, in May 1936, Stalin facilitated the establishment throughout the USSR of 'Obshchestvennitsa' – 'the housewives' movement' – that, according to historian Mary Buckley, was comprised of "public spirited women … who laboured without pay in hostels, canteens, nurseries, kindergartens, schools, hospitals, factories, offices and mines … supporting husbands in the labour force in a range of ways".[47]

Stalin was more than content for women to fill vacancies in the new industrial facilities built as a result of the latest Five-Year Plan – after all, a war economy was being created from 1936 onwards – and propaganda encouraged women to take jobs in industry. A huge increase in the number of day care facilities, crèches, nursery schools and laundries helped women to return to work much sooner than they would have done, otherwise. In 1928, only 3 million women in the USSR were industrial workers; by 1936, the figure was 9 million; and by 1941, more than 13 million women were working in Soviet industry.

In short, women in Stalin's USSR had two important roles: the first was as mothers who produced plenty of children that would grow up to be workers or soldiers; the second as members of a reserve labour force that was helping to power the new Soviet industrial economy.

CONSOLIDATE YOUR KNOWLEDGE

8. What were Stalin's main aims in the field of education?
9. What were the main weaknesses of Stalin's education system?
10. Describe two of the important education reforms that Stalin introduced. Briefly describe the effects of those reforms.
11. Following Stalin's reforms, was the Soviet education system more effective by 1941? Give reasons for your answer.
12. What roles did Stalin envisage for women? What objectives lay behind his approach?
13. Outline two of Stalin's policies which altered the role of women.
14. Why did Stalin feel that women should take up jobs in industry?
15. In what ways did the Soviet government help mothers who wanted to return to work?

TASK

Copy out the table below and summarise the impact Stalin's policies had on the role of women in the following areas.

Women	Impact of Stalin's policies
Legal rights	
In the home	
In the workforce	
In the Party	

Religion and the position of the Church

Under Lenin, the Russian Orthodox Church had been subjected to fierce persecution by Bolsheviks [see p.92], and Stalin continued this approach.

In 1928, the Bolshevik regime had turned its attention to Islam, closing many mosques and restricting Islamic customs, notably in the USSR's Central Asian republics. Stalin also launched a fresh wave of persecution against the Orthodox Church, which had retained much of its pre-Revolutionary influence in rural areas. From 1929, all churches and congregations had to be registered with the government and the Church was banned from engaging in educational activities – in fact, in many ways, in the education system of the USSR and in youth organisations, religion had been replaced by the glories of the Revolution, by the figures of Lenin and Stalin, and by the idea of the common good. The Stalinist regime had used propaganda incredibly effectively in further reducing the influence of organised religion.

As a way to promote atheism, the Communist Party had, in 1925, established the League of Militant Atheists – which, as historian Daniel Peris explains, "sponsored lectures, organised demonstrations and actively propagandised against religious observance"[48] – and by the late 1930s, it claimed to have more than five million members. At the same time, and particularly during collectivisation, Komsomol members would also carry out attacks on churches, priests and lay organisers, especially in the countryside.

In the 1930s, hundreds of churches were burned down or demolished, and during the Great Terror (1936–39) roughly 800 senior clergymen and about 4,000 priests were imprisoned, along with many lay members of the Church. In 1914, there had been about 55,000 churches, and almost 30,000 private chapels serving institutions, country estates and so on, but by 1940, only about 500 churches remained open. Religious activity did continue – it was much harder for the state to eradicate religious beliefs, especially among older people and people in rural areas – but, under Stalin, people were forced to worship largely in secret.

CONSOLIDATE YOUR KNOWLEDGE

16. What was the League of Militant Atheists?
17. Why did many clergy become victims of Stalin's purges in the 1930s?
18. How did the position of the Russian Orthodox Church change between 1928 and 1941?

Conclusions

The period between 1928 and 1941 was one of unprecedented economic upheaval. It was also one of radical social change, partly as a result of Stalin's cultural revolution. The Stalinist state created by 1941 controlled almost every aspect of everyday life, including forms of culture and even leisure activities.

The influence of religion had further declined and the education system had been transformed. The position of women, having changed under Lenin, had changed again to reflect Stalin's vision. Stalin's new society was a totalitarian dictatorship, controlled by his party and his officials.

CONSOLIDATE YOUR KNOWLEDGE

19. Explain the cultural values of Stalinist Russia by 1941.

GROUP ACTIVITY

As a group, and using your own knowledge and research, explain how Stalin used culture as a means of control over the USSR and its people between 1924 and 1941.

Discuss and present your findings.

Revision Section: Stalin in Power, 1924–41

This section will give a summary of the main events and developments during Stalin's rise to power and the creation of a totalitarian state under his control. It is important to understand the impact of these events on society, on government and on the economy in the USSR. To help students prepare for assessments and unit tests there will be some brief summaries of these key events – which should help to underline their importance and consolidate knowledge – along with a few sample exam questions.

Independent research on the main figures and decisions of the period between 1924 and 1941 will also help improve in understanding Stalin's aims and actions as he created and presided over a totalitarian dictatorship

Turning point 1: Stalin's rise to power, 1917–24

At the time of the Revolution and, in fact, for some time afterwards, Stalin was not one of the better-known Bolshevik leaders. Students must be able to explain how, between the October Revolution of 1917 and Lenin's death in January 1924, Stalin laid the foundations for his assumption of political power. Students also need to display a clear awareness of the means by which he acquired complete control of the party and the country after Lenin's death.

Stalin establishes a sizeable power base, 1917–24

1917
- Stalin becomes commissar for nationalities.

1919
- Key central parts of the Communist Party are established, namely the Politburo, the Orgburo and the Secretariat.
- Stalin oversees the day-to-day, operational work of the Politburo.
- Stalin is the only person who is a member of all three bodies.

April
- Stalin appointed commissar of The Workers' and Peasants' Inspectorate.

1922

April
- Stalin appointed general secretary of the Communist Party.

December
- The USSR is established.

1922–24
- Lenin becomes increasingly incapacitated.
- The *troika* (triumvirate) of Stalin, Kamenev and Zinoviev, takes control of the USSR.

1923–25
- 'Lenin Enrolment' boosts party membership, which aids Stalin and his allies.

155

Turning point 2: The power struggle, 1924–29

First, Stalin removed his most obvious political rivals (Trotsky, Kamenev and Zinoviev). By 1926, he had neutralised the Left and was ready to tackle the Right of the party.

There were three main phases in this power struggle, during which disagreements over policy divided party members. The weaknesses of his rivals, their often personal divisions, and their disputes over policies worked to Stalin's advantage, and by 1929 he had emerged as the victor of the power struggle. When Stalin's opponents were removed from the Politburo, they were replaced with loyal Stalinists.

LEFT				RIGHT		
Trotsky	Kamenev	Zinoviev		Bukharin	Rykov	Tomsky
STALIN						

Phase 1, 1924–5: The triumvirate vs Trotsky

Issues   Lenin's Testament

NEP

Permanent Revolution

Bureaucratisation

Phase 2, 1925–6: United Opposition (or Left) vs Stalin and the Right

Issues   NEP

Permanent Revolution

Socialism in one country

Bureaucratisation

Phase 3, 1928–9: Stalin vs the Right

Issues   End of NEP

Five-year plans

Collectivisation

By 1929, Stalin's political rivals had been marginalised. He then set about creating a totalitarian state in the USSR and had achieved that aim, well before 1941.

Turning point 3: Stalinist terror, 1934–41

There is no doubt that the purges and state terror did a lot of harm to the USSR. Estimates vary, and official records are incomplete and inaccurate, however it is likely that approximately 20 million lives were lost in this period, if all forms of oppression – including famines deliberately induced by the regime – are taken into account.

Stalin purged the party and the armed forces (including the Red Army). Ordinary citizens were targeted, if the regime felt they were members of hostile or potentially hostile groups. He even purged the secret police. Stalin's control over the USSR, underpinned by his personality cult and extensive use of propaganda, was reinforced by the purges.

Reasons for the purges

- Kirov was a potential rival to Stalin and his murder in 1934 led to the purges.
- The Old Bolsheviks were eliminated.
- Any other potential sources of opposition within the party were removed.
- Stalin was able to achieve an even greater degree of control over the party, the armed forces and workers.
- People were more likely to be loyal to the regime, even in private (in case they were betrayed by relatives or friends).

Effects of the purges

- Approximately 20 million lives were lost.
- Most Old Bolsheviks were executed.
- Many army officers (and generals in particular) were executed.
- Some secret police leaders were purged.
- The resistance of peasants to Stalin's policies was eliminated.
- Workers were brought under closer state control.
- By 1939 a 'terror state' was created.
- Stalin's hold on power, already quite strong, was even more assured.

PRACTICE EXAMINATION QUESTIONS, 1924–41

Based on format of questions for CCEA Unit AS2, Option 5 (Russia).

These questions are for individual or class-based use and study. Questions from past papers and specimen papers can be accessed through the CCEA GCE History microsite.

www.rewardinglearning.org.uk/microsites/history/gce/past_papers/index.asp

These are some sample 8-mark and 22-mark examination-type questions, to help students to prepare and practice for assessment tasks for this period.

8-mark questions (short responses)

a) Explain Stalin's political aims in 1924.

b) Explain the strengths of Stalin's political position in 1924.

c) Explain the weaknesses of Trotsky's political position in 1924.

d) Explain the main features of Stalin's cult of personality in the 1930s.

e) Explain how Stalin was able to defeat Trotsky by 1927.

f) Explain Stalin's cultural aims for the Soviet Union between 1924 and 1941.

g) Explain why Stalin carried out the purges between 1934 and 1939.

22-mark questions (essay answers)

- "Divisions within the Communist Party were the most important factor in determining Stalin's success in the struggle for party control between 1922 and 1929." How valid do you believe that statement to be?

- To what extent was Stalin's control of the party the most important reason for his victory in the power struggle between 1922 and 1929?

- How far would you agree that Stalin's use of the cult of personality was the most important basis of his control over the USSR between 1929 and 1941?

- "Stalin's use of terror was the main basis of his political power within the USSR between 1929 and 1941." How far would you accept this statement?

Endnotes

1. Laver, John, *Joseph Stalin – From Revolutionary to Despot* (Hodder, 1993) p.26

2. Ibid, p.1

3. Rigby, Thomas Henry, *Stalin* (Prentice-Hall, 1966), p.39

4. *See* Reed, John, *Ten Days That Shook the World* (Penguin, 1977)

5. Laver, *Joseph Stalin,* p.17

6. Rigby, *Stalin,* p.96

7. *From* McCauley, Martin, *The Rise and Fall of the Soviet Union* (Routledge, 2013), p.485

8. Figes, Orlando, *Revolutionary Russia, 1891–1991: A History* (Metropolitan, 2014), p.173

9. *From* Lee, Stephen J., *Europe, 1890-1945* (Routledge, 2003), p.278

10. Tumarkin, Nina, *Lenin Lives!: The Lenin Cult in Soviet Russia* (Harvard University Press, 1997), p.113

11. Carr, E.H., *The Russian Revolution: From Lenin to Stalin, 1917–1929* (Palgrave Macmillan, 2004), p.70

12. Lenin's attitude towards Stalin had changed, partly because Stalin had been rude and abusive towards Lenin's wife Nadezhda on more than one occasion.

13. Laver, *Joseph Stalin,* p.23

14. Lenin, V.I., *Collected Works, Volume 36* (Lawrence & Wishart, 1966) p.595

15. Ibid. p.595

16. *From* Ascher, Abraham, *Stalin,* eBook (Oneworld Publications, 2016)

17. Figes, *Revolutionary Russia,* p.181

18. North, David, *In Defense of Leon Trotsky* (Mehring Books, 2010) p.78

19. Trotsky, Leon and Wright, John G. (translator) 'The Lessons of October', *Collected Works, Volume 3* (Pioneer Publishers, 1937)

20. Service, Robert, *Trotsky: A Biography* (Macmillan, 2009) p.95.

21. Between 1923 and 1926, the Politburo had had just six members in practice

22. Trotsky went first to Turkey, then France, Norway and finally, Mexico. However external exile provoked ever harsher criticism of Stalin, and in 1940 he was assassinated by Soviet agents.

23. *From* Lee, Stephen J., *European Dictatorships, 1918–1945* (4th ed. Routledge, 2016) p.56

24. Rayfield, Donald, *Stalin and His Hangmen: An Authoritative Portrait of a Tyrant and Those Who Served Him,* eBook (Penguin, 2005)

25. McCauley, Martin, *Stalin and Stalinism* (3rd ed. Routledge, 2013), p.34

26. The full name of the secret police from 1923–34 translates to the Joint State Political Directorate. In Russian this abbreviates to OGPU.

27. Figes, *Revolutionary Russia,* p.232

28. Ibid. p.222

29. *From* Plamper, Jan, *The Stalin Cult: A Study in the Alchemy of Power* (Yale University Press, 2012) p.64

30. Central Executive Committee, 'On the Amendment of the Criminal Procedural Codes of the Union Republics', 1 December 1934

31. Yagoda had actually held effective control over the OGPU since 1924, although more senior Bolsheviks had been in charge.

32. Resolution of Politburo on 'Measures for Protecting the USSR from infiltration of spies, terrorist and diversion elements', 9 March 1936

33. Davies, Sarah and James Harris, *Stalin: A New History* (Cambridge University Press, 2005)

34. This is the name of Schapiro's chapter on the purges. *From* Schapiro, Leonard, *The Communist Party of the Soviet Union* (Eyre & Spottiswoode, 1960)

35. *From* Fitzpatrick, Sheila, *The Russian Revolution* (Oxford University Press, 1994), p.166

36. *From* Laver, *Joseph Stalin,* p.43

37. Rappaport, Helen, *Joseph Stalin: A Biographical Companion*, (ABC CLIO, 1999), p.118

38. Fitzpatrick, *Russian Revolution*, p.169

39. Phillips, Steve, *Stalinist Russia (*Heinemann, 2000) p.56

40. Party Central Committee, 'On the reconstruction of literary-artistic organizations', 23 April 1932

41. Rappaport, *Joseph Stalin*, p.81

42. Fitzpatrick, *Russian Revolution*, p.181

43. Butler, Rupert, *Stalin's Secret Police: A History of the CHEKA, OGPU, NKVD, SMERSH & KGB, 1917–1991*, eBook (Amber Books, 2017)

44. Figes, Orlando, *Revolutionary Russia, 1891–1991: A History* (Metropolitan, 2014), p.260

45. Membership was not compulsory, but those who failed to join often found it very difficult to pursue higher education.

46. 'Decree on the Prohibition of Abortions', 27 June 1936

47. Buckley, Mary, 'The Untold Story of the Obshchestvennitsa in the 1930s', Ilič, Melanie, (ed) *Women in the Stalin Era. Studies in Russian and East European History and Society* (Palgrave Macmillan, 2001) pp.151–2

48. Peris, Daniel, *Storming the Heavens: The Soviet League of the Militant Godless* (Cornell University Press, 1998). p.2

STALIN AND THE SOVIET ECONOMY
1924–41

This chapter will examine:

4.1: The aims and degrees of success of Stalin's economic policies by 1928.

4.2: The aims and features of collectivisation and its effects on agriculture.

4.3: The policy of Industrialisation and the series of Five-Year Plans, including an assessment of their aims and levels of success.

4.4: The social impact of Stalin's economic policies on the USSR and its citizens by 1941.

At the end of this chapter there will be a summary of the causes and effects of some of the key events in this period, along with some exam-style questions.

4.1: Stalin and the Economy, 1924–28

In 1924, when Stalin emerged as the USSR's new leader, he inherited Lenin's economic policies and, broadly speaking, upheld them for several years – after all, the consolidation of political power was his main priority. In 1928–9, however, in the belief that much more extreme economic policies were needed in order to industrialise the USSR, Stalin began to introduce his own policies, including 'Socialism in one Country', the first Five-Year Plan and collectivisation.

The continuing problem of the NEP

In the aftermath of the civil war and War Communism, Lenin had instituted the NEP as a temporary solution to Russia's economic problems [see p.81]. This policy had led to improvements in both industrial and agricultural output, but by 1924 the production levels for both these areas were still insufficient – they could not support a long-term programme of economic modernisation in the USSR.

Another weakness of the NEP was a political one. In the opinion of some party members, the NEP had helped to enrich the 'capitalist bourgeoisie'. The main targets of their anger were groups like the kulaks (the better-off peasants) and the NEPmen (the class of small traders that had sprung up because of the NEP).

By 1924, the NEP had also not solved two of Russia's long-term economic problems: the problem of peasant rights and land reform; and the limited scale of industrialisation in the USSR. The country's inability to produce many of the products it needed made it dependent on imports from hostile Western governments.

After Lenin's death, the debate over the future of the Soviet economy turned into another intense battle within the party. Stalin was no economic expert and he avoided taking sides as the party argued over future economic policies. Although he formed alliances of convenience – firstly with Zinoviev and Kamenev against Trotsky; and then with Bukharin and Rykov against the Left – he managed to remain above the economic debate between 1924 and 1928.

Bukharin and the Right wanted to continue the NEP They felt that it would preserve prosperity, allowing Russia to produce the food and basic household goods it needed, and would keep taxes low. In theory at least, the peasants would sell their produce to the government and, in turn, the government would exchange the goods for desperately needed foreign currency.

Trotsky and the Left opposed this approach to the NEP They argued that the NEP must be brought to an end so that a fully socialist economy could be created. They criticised Bukharin's plans, claiming that they would not provide the state with enough capital to finance their desired expansion into manufacturing. The Left argued that Communist Party leaders would have to impose a programme of rapid industrial growth, which would make higher taxes on peasants necessary.

CONSOLIDATE YOUR KNOWLEDGE

1. Explain why the NEP was so popular in 1924.
2. Why did some party members oppose the NEP, particularly after 1924?
3. Which groups in Soviet society benefited from the NEP?
4. What were Stalin's main economic aims in 1924?
5. Outline Bukharin's economic policies in 1924?

Stalin's economic aims, 1924–28

To Stalin, the continuing poor harvests of the 1920s highlighted the need to deal with the peasantry, once and for all. In 1925, he presented his vision of building Socialism in One Country – the strengthening of the Soviet Union through far-reaching modernisation of the whole country, using its own raw materials and other resources.

Protecting the legacy of the Bolshevik revolution at home was much more important to Stalin than the spread of world revolution (something that Trotsky had advocated). Trotsky attacked Stalin's new approach to the economy but did not have much support. Most people believed that the continuation of the NEP went hand in hand with Socialism in One Country.

Stalin also believed that economic reform was essential for the USSR to increase its military strength, in order to defend the Revolution against its capitalist enemies. For the USSR to become a modern, industrial power, its system of agriculture had to become much more efficient. Otherwise, it would not be able to feed larger numbers of factory workers or supply certain raw materials that industry would need.

By 1928, Stalin believed that only radical economic change could transform the USSR into a socialist society with a modern industrial base.

CONSOLIDATE YOUR KNOWLEDGE

6. In the opinion of Stalin and his supporters, how would Socialism in One Country solve the economic problems of the USSR?
7. Why did Trotsky oppose Stalin's economic policies by 1928?
8. What were Stalin's economic aims by 1928?
9. What was Socialism in One Country?

The need for economic change by 1928

Stalin had decided to make large-scale industrialisation his top priority for the USSR in order to:

- Increase grain supplies, especially after yet another poor harvest in 1927.
- Increase industrial production.
- Develop new industries.
- Strengthen his political position.
- Improve living standards of workers and peasants.
- Strengthen the defence forces of the USSR.
- Defeat Bukharin and the Right opposition.
- Defeat Trotsky and the Left – which he had done by 1928.
- Replace NEP, which he felt had failed to boost industrial production to the extent he wanted.

Russia's economic underdevelopment was the greatest source of Stalin's problems. Marxist theory suggested that only industrialisation could lead to the revolutionary transformation of society, yet throughout Russia's history peasants had made up the vast bulk of the population and their loyalty to the Communist regime was in doubt. Stalin's post-1928 economic policies reduced the influence and independence of peasants by virtually wiping out the kulaks as a recognisable group This greatly increased the number of people who lived in urban areas and were employed in manufacturing.

In the 1920s, the Communist Party was politically and ideologically committed to the economic modernisation of the USSR, however members disagreed about the means. The key question facing Stalin and the party in 1928 was whether the process should be gradual (and the NEP allowed to continue) or whether the pace of economic change should be accelerated (and the NEP replaced). Certainly, some party members had been strongly opposed to the NEP's capitalist elements for years, but this was not Stalin's motive for change: he genuinely wanted the USSR to be transformed, economically, under his leadership.

Stalin had already advocated a series of Five-Year Plans with the aim of modernising the economy (though this in itself did not mean an end for the NEP), but to achieve the sort of change he believed would be necessary, he decided to adopt the policies of the, now-defeated, Left (led by Trotsky, Kamenev and Zinoviev). Historians have sometimes called this 'Stalin's left turn'. The manoeuvre had been prompted by growing divisions within the party when, in 1927, another economic crisis was blamed on the NEP.

That year, in an effort to encourage peasants to produce more grain, the prices of most consumer goods had been cut, however, that led to chronic food shortages in urban areas. During this economic crisis, the secret police (the OGPU) had clamped down on the black market and speculators. At the time of the 1927 harvest, grain prices were reduced but food supplies fell again. Factory and office workers, the people who were expected to build the new USSR, found that less food was available. Some party leaders accused kulaks of hoarding grain and advocated class war as an alternative to the NEP Peasants were blamed for delaying industrialisation but Bukharin and the Right argued that the peasants were not yet ready for Communism.

In December 1927, at the 15th Party Congress, Stalin revealed his proposal for agricultural Five-Year Plans, based on the collectivisation of farms [covered in section 4.2]. He felt that collectivisation would solve the food-supply problems and support an industrial revolution in the USSR.

In 1928 Stalin ended the NEP, acting against Bukharin and the Right Opposition when he introduced his new economic policies. He justified this decision in a speech to managers of industry in February 1931:

Do you want our socialist fatherland to be beaten and to lose its independence? If you do not want this, you must put an end to its backwardness in the shortest possible time and develop a genuine Bolshevik tempo in building up its socialist economy.[1]

CONSOLIDATE YOUR KNOWLEDGE

10. Why was the 1927 crisis over the NEP so politically important?

11. What were Stalin's two main economic problems in 1928?

12. What were the political effects of Stalin's decision to abandon the NEP?

13. Why did Stalin want to introduce his own economic policies in 1928?

GROUP ACTIVITY

As a group, and using your own knowledge and research, explain why, according to Marxist ideology, the Soviet economy had to change. What obstacles hindered this change by 1928?

Discuss and present your findings.

4.2: Collectivisation and Agriculture, 1928–41

Key dates and events, 1929–41

1929		First Five-Year Plan approved by party congress. Large-scale collectivisation made compulsory and enforced.
1932		Second Five-Year Plan published (implemented between January 1933 and December 1937)
1934	December	Kirov is assassinated Start of the great purges
1936	August	Show trials of Kamenev, Zinoviev and minor allies
1938	March	Show trials of Bukharin, Rykov, Yagoda and allies
1939	August	The Nazi-Soviet Pact is signed.
	September	Partition of Poland between USSR and Germany
1941	June	German invasion of USSR (Operation Barbarossa)

The aims of collectivisation

At the 1926 Party Congress, Stalin had promised to "transform our country from an agrarian one into an industrial one".[2] However, to achieve this aim, he would first have to solve a problem that had previously defeated Lenin and even (before the First World War) the tsarist prime minister, Stolypin – the problem of peasants, agricultural productivity and land reform.

At the time, agriculture in the USSR still relied on very small farms, most of which were owned by peasants. There was little mechanisation of any kind and modern agricultural theories were not well understood. For reasons such as those, Soviet agriculture was extremely inefficient and unproductive. Throughout the 1920s, peasants were not supplying enough food to the existing number of industrial workers, let alone the expanded urban industrial labour force envisaged under the Five-Year Plans. In Lenin's time, the industrial workforce had grown and, although the NEP remained in place until 1928, that expansion was in line with Stalin's vision of Socialism in One Country. However, the USSR's food-production capacity did not increase by enough to feed all factory workers.

Party unity on economic policy was comprehensively shattered at the Central Committee meeting in July 1928, which followed the 1927–28 crisis in agriculture [see p.167]. Stalin led demands for cheap grain in order to make his Five-Year Plans for economic development feasible – he and his supporters were of the opinion that the only way to attain that objective was to challenge the power and privileges of the peasantry. Bukharin opposed that approach, calling instead for an increase in trade between rural and urban areas, to spread economic development more evenly throughout the USSR. Stalin and his supporters called Bukharin's plans 'defeatist'. Stalin felt that he had no option but to move against the Right of the party and to bring peasants firmly under state control.

Stalin blamed the kulaks for causing this agricultural crisis. In a speech on agrarian policy on 27 December 1929, he declared, "We have passed from the policy of restricting … the kulaks, to the policy of eliminating the kulaks as a class."[3] In 1928 he had granted emergency powers to the authorities, which allowed them to collect grain by force from the kulaks and 'middle peasants', who had occasionally withheld some of what they produced because they were unhappy about the management of the economy and the unavailability of consumer goods. 'Procurement squads' were sent out to coerce the peasantry and were told to use whatever means they felt to be necessary. The idea was that the often unrealistic grain production targets set by the party would be reached simply by seizing as much as the government wanted.

It was a form of class warfare imposed by the government – and a partial return to the policies of War Communism – which alienated most peasants (not just the kulaks). In many rural areas, there was economic chaos. Within the party, there was more tension between Stalin's supporters and those of the Right Opposition who felt that Stalin was recreating some of the economic conditions that had existed during the civil war.

The answer, Stalin felt, was collectivisation and the end of the NEP Collectivisation would bring small farms together in groups to create larger units – *kolkhozy* (state farms)[4] – which, the government hoped, would be much more efficient. More machinery (such as tractors and threshers) would be used in order to increase food production and the new collective farms would be less labour intensive. Having been freed from their traditional roles in the fields, many peasants would be able to take up jobs in factories. In that way, the most important objective of Stalin's Five-Year Plans, that of industrialisation, would be met and the future economic success of the USSR assured (in theory more than practice).

Collectivisation wasn't a new policy or idea: Lenin had considered introducing it during the civil war to deal with the land problem. Stalin saw it as a permanent solution to one of Russia's longest-running problems: a way to deal with the peasants, once and for all. In 1928, the party had introduced collectivisation on a voluntary basis and some peasants did support it, setting up a small number of collective farms – though these had limited success.

Stalin and his supporters remained convinced that it was an economic and political necessity to transform the Soviet Union, and in 1929 collectivisation became official government policy.

CONSOLIDATE YOUR KNOWLEDGE

1. Why had Lenin been unable to solve the problem of the peasantry by 1924?
2. Why did Stalin want to introduce collectivisation in 1928?
3. Why did Bukharin and his supporters oppose Stalin's plans?
4. Who did Stalin blame for the agrarian crisis of 1928? Why did he do so?
5. Why was there so much opposition to collectivisation from the peasantry?
6. How, according to Stalin, would collectivisation solve several economic problems?
7. Why was the success of the system of Five-Year Plans dependent on collectivisation to some extent?

Stalin and collectivisation

In September 1929, Stalin made collectivisation compulsory. The imposition of the policy was overseen by local party officials loyal to Stalin. Kulaks were not allowed to become involved with the new collective farms and in the autumn and early winter of 1929, many were deported to bleak and remote regions (such as Siberia and the Ural Mountains). They had been effectively eliminated as a class by the state.

During 1929, the number of collective farms rose until they made up 15 per cent of all farms in the USSR (prior to this, they had made up only 7.4 per cent). By March 1930 people from 11 million Soviet households were working on collective farms. By 1932, 62 per cent of peasant households had been 'collectivised'; and by 1937, the figure had risen to 97 per cent.

Stalin and Soviet propaganda presented the policy of collectivisation as a great success but, in reality, the party had imposed it on peasants and most of them had been strongly resistant. In fact, the opposition was often violent. That was particularly true in the Caucasus and the Ukraine, known as 'Russia's breadbasket' since it had the best agricultural land. The regime dealt with such opposition by establishing 'dekulakisation' squads, which were comprised of party members. About 25,000 party members from urban areas were sent to rural areas to root out resistance, backed by the secret police (the OGPU) and the Red Army.

So great was the level of resistance that in 1930 Stalin called a temporary halt to collectivisation, justifying this short-lived change of policy in his famous 'Dizzy with Success' speech – an address delivered to factory managers and reported in *Pravda* on 2 March 1930 – in which he asserted that the problems experienced "could have arisen only because some of our comrades have become dizzy with success".[5]

However, after a short break of just a few months, Stalin resumed his policy on collectivisation, and it was enforced even more rigorously than it had been before.

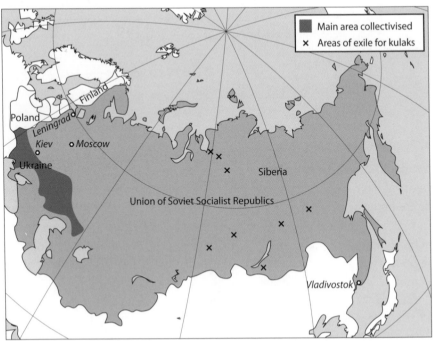

The main areas of the USSR collectivised by 1932, and the places of exile for kulaks.

CONSOLIDATE YOUR KNOWLEDGE

8. Why did Stalin make collectivisation compulsory in 1929?

9. What effects did this new policy have on the peasants by 1932?

10. Describe the main features of collectivisation.

11. Why did the Soviet regime claim that collectivisation had been a great success?

12. How did Stalin deal with opposition to collectivisation?

Peasants marching in support of collectivisation, 1932. The banner reads: "We, as kolkhozniks, will eradicate the kulaks, following the total collectivisation principle".

The effects of collectivisation by 1933

Under collectivisation, peasants were not only forced to hand over their land, but also their animals and even their hand tools, which left them with nothing. Determined that their property would not be given to Stalin's government, many peasants chose to set fire to their houses and barns, and to slaughter their animals. Some also defied the regime by refusing to sow cereal crops, the most important of which were corn (maize) and wheat.

The party and state institutions were relentless in their response to this resistance. The kulaks were shot or forced into internal exile. Terror was used on a widespread scale in an attempt to ensure that enough food would be produced for the growing number of factory workers. It wasn't unusual for people who stole grain to be shot. In some cases, their families were shot too, as no resistance was tolerated by the Stalinist state.

Between 1928 and 1933, the number of heads of cattle was halved and cereal production declined sharply [see table below[6]]. Procurement targets for cereals were achieved only through confiscation and the threat or use of force. In 1932, the grain quotas demanded by the authorities in the Ukraine were raised by over 40 per cent. This left little or no surplus grain for millions of peasants once the party officials had collected the new quotas.

Product	1930	1931	1932	1933
Sheep and goats (millions)	108.8	77.7	52.1	50.2
Grain harvest (million tons)	83.5	69.5	69.6	68.4
Cattle (millions)	52.5	47.9	40.7	38.4
State procurements (million tons)	22.1	22.8	18.5	22.6
Pigs (millions)	13.6	14.4	11.6	12.1

Agricultural production during collectivisation, 1930–33.

Thanks to the effects of collectivisation, along with the bad harvest of 1932–33, there was a massive fall in agricultural production, resulting in large-scale famines. Peasants were left to starve to death and some even resorted to cannibalism to survive. In the end, about 10 million peasants lost their lives.

Despite this, the Soviet propaganda machine continued to tell the world that collectivisation had been a great success for the Soviet Union and for Stalin. As with so many Communist Party schemes, the truth was that it had damaged the economy and even the agricultural sector itself.

CONSOLIDATE YOUR KNOWLEDGE

13. Why was terror needed to crush peasant opposition?
14. What effects did collectivisation have on the kulaks?
15. In what ways did peasants resist collectivisation?
16. What were the two most important effects that collectivisation had on the Soviet economy by 1933?

TASK

Create a spider diagram that lists the effects of collectivism. Which of these was the most important in your opinion?

Role of the peasants

By 1933, many Soviet citizens had paid a very heavy price for collectivisation. Despite that, the authorities continued to maintain that collectivisation was of great benefit. Reports of famine, which appeared in the Western media from time to time, were strenuously denied, which meant that no international appeal for help could be made (unlike during the period of civil war).

And this famine had been avoidable since, throughout the period, the USSR had continued to export grain in order to obtain the foreign currency it needed to support the industrialisation programmes of the first Five-Year Plan (mainly through the purchase of foreign-made machinery). Historian Isaac Deutscher described it as "the first man-made famine in history"[7]

Peasants failed to see any justification, ideological or economic, for collectivisation despite Soviet propaganda stressing its benefits. After the famines of 1932 and 1933, Stalin was forced to make concessions. Peasants were offered incentives if they agreed to work on collective farms. For instance, they were allowed to have their own private plots of around one acre, and to keep or sell whatever they could produce on those smallholdings. This proved to be popular and, remarkably, helped agriculture recover. By 1937, these small plots accounted for 52 per cent of potato and vegetable production and 71 per cent of meat and milk production.

CONSOLIDATE YOUR KNOWLEDGE

17. What were the causes of the famine in parts of the USSR by 1932–33?
18. Why did the Soviet regime deny the existence of this famine, when reports appeared in newspapers in the Western world?
19. How was propaganda used in support of collectivisation?
20. Why was Stalin forced to take a more moderate approach to collectivisation and peasants, after 1933?

The effects of collectivisation by 1941

By 1939, almost all farms in the USSR had been collectivised and there were more than 250,000 *kolkhozy* (state farms). The peasants had been coerced into the collective-farm system, but the government had then found it necessary to appease them.

Women threshing on a collective farm, *c*.1930.

Many farms underwent a good deal of mechanisation, due largely to the Machine and Tractor Stations (MTS). These were established all over the country and they provided collective farms with both machinery and people to operate the new technology. This meant that millions of peasants were no longer required for manual labour in the fields. They were now available for work in factories and so were gradually moved into urban areas, while those left in rural areas, having been brought under the control of the state, were now wage slaves, just like their urban counterparts. Approximately 15 million kulaks, once seen as a threat to the state, had been completely neutralised.

The effects of collectivisation can be divided into three broad categories – economic, political and social:

Economic
- Grain supplies requisitioned using force.
- More use made of machinery (e.g. tractors).
- Creation of large collective farms (*kolkhozy*).
- Fall in livestock numbers.
- Severe food shortages and famine.
- Agriculture failed to make any significant progress.

Political
- Rural areas brought more firmly under control of Soviet authorities and the party.
- Internal passports introduced in 1932 to restrict travel by peasants.
- Collectivisation used as means of state control.
- Agriculture based on socialist methods.

Social
- Kulaks removed, and most eliminated.
- Women able to play a greater role in agriculture on collective farms.
- Villages now administered by the local collective farm.
- Kolkhoz chairman appointed by the party.
- Peasant-controlled office of mayor abolished.
- Greater provision of education in rural areas.
- Higher rates of literacy.

Conclusions

Stalin claimed that collectivisation was a success but, despite his efforts in the 1930s, Soviet agricultural figures still barely matched those of the tsarist government in 1913. The enormous stresses that collectivisation had placed on Soviet agriculture and society had, in reality, left the country in poor condition and unprepared for the Second World War (which the USSR joined in June 1941) as farmers struggled to feed the expanding urban workforce and the armed forces.

Under collectivisation, economic progress had been modest and the human cost very high. Millions of people died because of Stalin's ideological experiment. Others were stripped of all their property, sent hundreds (or thousands) of miles from their homes and made to work in factories, or even labour camps. Those who stayed behind in the countryside had become employees of the state – reduced to the status of latter-day serfs.

Agricultural productivity, the very problem collectivisation was meant to solve, dropped between 1929 and 1941. While peasants starved, Stalin allowed cereal exports to continue to earn money for his industrialisation programmes. Farmers lost their own equipment and, at first, there was not enough machinery to work the new collective farms. The most productive agricultural group, the kulaks, had been destroyed. Farming was thereafter in the hands of party and state officials, not experienced farmers. As historian Orlando Figes explains:

> The collective farms were a dismal failure. They never really worked. In the early years, few had tractors to replace the horses slaughtered by the peasantry … They were badly run by managers appointed for their loyalty to the state rather than their agricultural expertise.[8]

However from Stalin's perspective, collectivisation had been extremely successful in one sense at least: through it he had finally eliminated the threat the peasant class had posed to the regime. Over 25 million family farms had been replaced by 250,000 collective farms and at long last, the party controlled the countryside.

CONSOLIDATE YOUR KNOWLEDGE

21. What effects did collectivisation have on the economy up until 1939?
22. How important were the Machinery and Tractor Stations in the functioning of collective farms?
23. Why was there no real improvement in agricultural production figures between 1929 and 1939?
24. How did collectivisation leave the economy badly prepared for war?
25. What was the human cost of collectivisation?

GROUP ACTIVITY

Organise a class debate with the motion:

"Collectivisation was a successful economic policy for Stalin between 1929 and 1941."

TASK

Copy table below and include examples of positive and negative effects of collectivisation upon the Soviet economy by 1941. Add more rows as necessary.

Positive effects	Negative effects

4.3: Industry and the Five-Year Plans, 1928–41

Alongside the agricultural revolution, was a parallel revolution in industry. In 1928, Russian industry was still underdeveloped and confined mostly to the areas surrounding Moscow and Leningrad – transformation was undoubtedly necessary if the USSR's economy was to be modernised.

In 1925, when Stalin had first advocated Socialism in One Country, he had suggested that this might be achieved using the NEP However, shortly before the first of the Five-Year Plans was launched, Stalin argued that the NEP was holding back the industrial growth necessary to create the sort of country he envisaged. By changing his position, Stalin was also able to justify the marginalisation of Bukharin and the Right Opposition [see p.128].

In 1927, the Soviet government began laying the groundwork for large projects in the steel and armaments industries, on the railways, and in electricity generation (which, at that time, was dominated by massive hydro-electric schemes). These would provide the foundations for future industrial expansion under Stalin's Five-Year Plans.

There were three Five-Year Plans in the period between 1928 and 1941, though these often did not run for the full five years. They were overseen by a revamped Gosplan – the State Planning Committee (responsible for detailed central planning of the economy) – which was controlled by the Communist Party. Gosplan set targets for industries and allocated resources.

The Five-Year Plans

First plan: October 1928–December 1932
Second plan: January 1933–December 1937
Third plan: January 1938–June 1941

CONSOLIDATE YOUR KNOWLEDGE

1. Why was collectivisation needed to help the Five-Year Plans reach their targets?
2. According to Stalin, how would the Five-Year Plans build Socialism in One Country?
3. What were the main functions of Gosplan after 1928?

The first Five-Year Plan, 1928–32

Aims of the first Five-Year Plan

The first of the Five-Year Plans was drawn up in 1927, promoted by Soviet propaganda in the autumn of 1928 – citizens were told that their efforts in industry would help to build the socialist utopia, which Stalin promised to create – and launched in October 1928. The party did not officially adopt it until the 16th Party Congress in April 1929, though, under Stalin, it was not unusual for some aspects of economic policy to be implemented or amended before they had been formally adopted as official party policy.

Stalin wanted to transform the Soviet Union into a modern industrial state as quickly as possible, so the first Five-Year Plan set out ambitious targets for industrial growth. Coal production was to increase by 100 per cent; steel production was to increase by 200 per cent; and electricity production was to increase by over 300 per cent. In the meantime, new industrial areas, such as those in the Urals, were to be developed. The Soviet government planned to build new cities to house the new industrial workforce – millions of displaced peasants. The spread of collectivisation would, in theory, feed the expanded industrial workforce in towns and cities across the USSR.

Stalin's fear of invasion by the Western powers was another factor in his push for modernisation. A Soviet state backed by the might of modern industry would be able to resist any future military threat and, indeed, although the forces of Nazi Germany and its allies swept across the western USSR in 1941, Stalin's new Red Empire proved to be resilient. Stalin argued that rapid industrial growth was absolutely vital to the country's survival and he refused to tolerate any attempts

A Soviet poster promoting the first Five-Year Plan, 1928. The slogan reads, "Industrialisation is the road to socialism!"

to slow down industrialisation and collectivisation. In February 1931, in a speech to managers of Soviet industry, he said, "We are fifty or a hundred years behind the advanced countries. We must make good this distance in ten years. Either we do it, or we shall go under."[9]

Stalin saw steel and oil production as the main drivers of future economic growth and, of course, those are also the two most important industrial factors in a large-scale conventional war, so those industries were given priority, particularly under the first Five-Year Plan.

The targets set for all industries – the 'optimal quota' figures – tended to be unrealistic and were often amended or changed frequently, yet even the amended targets were often hopelessly divorced from economic reality [see table on page 185]. Of course, Stalin still punished party officials for failing to meet those targets.

CONSOLIDATE YOUR KNOWLEDGE

4. What were the main aims of the first Five-Year Plan?
5. What reasons did Stalin give in 1931 to justify the increased pace of industrialisation?
6. What industries were encouraged under the first Five-Year Plan and why?
7. Were the targets set for the first Five-Year Plan unrealistic in practice?

Effects of the first Five-Year Plan

The first Five-Year Plan involved economic change on an unprecedented scale. It created a planned socialist economy – a 'command economy' – through state-driven industrial growth. In 1930, the state declared private trade and employment illegal. All means of production in the USSR were to be controlled by the Communist state.

Stalin hoped to turn industrial workers into loyal Communists by convincing them of the benefits of the Five-Year Plans. The plans, it was argued, would help to raise living standards. In theory at least, opposition to the Five-Year Plan was not tolerated by the regime. In 1928 this led to the show trials of mining engineers accused of industrial sabotage.

When the first plan achieved some early successes, Stalin declared that it would become a four-year plan and would be completed by the end of 1932. "The Five-Year Plan in four!" was a propaganda slogan of the time.[10] Production targets for industry were revised upwards, yet again. Party volunteers, some of whom were teenage members of Komonsol, were encouraged to help build new industrial cities, such as Magnitogorsk, and by 1932, there were several new industrial zones across the USSR, such as the steelworks in Magnitogorsk, and the tractor factory in Kharkov. A contemporary slogan was "There are no fortresses we Bolsheviks cannot storm!"[11]

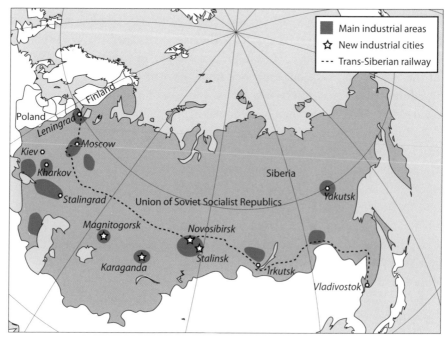

Industrial facilities created as a result of the Five-Year Plans.

In an effort to improve production figures and thereby meet the ambitious targets of the first Five-Year Plan, the Komonsol even asked its members to form 'shock worker brigades'. The party encouraged 'storming', where workers were pushed into making superhuman efforts, including being forced to work for twenty-four hours without a break. Industrial production was now treated as warfare: 'battles' were fought on an industrial 'front' by shock 'brigades' struggling with kulak 'resistance'. In a way, Soviet industrialisation was part of a struggle: the struggle between Stalin and his enemies (perceived or real), against whom the party and secret police had taken harsh measures.

By 1930, urban unemployment in the USSR had effectively disappeared.

Most of the members of this new industrial workforce were under the age of thirty and it is estimated that about 80 per cent had no relevant skills or experience. Between 1929 and 1932, more than nine million peasants moved to urban areas and became industrial workers. Millions of women had been recruited to the urban labour workforce by 1932. Slave labour, supplied by the Gulag organisation, was also used to build some of the industrial cities, hydro-electric projects and improved transport infrastructure across the USSR.

Millions of these new workers found that they were not well suited to some of the complex or physically demanding tasks they were expected to perform – they were, after all, mainly unskilled peasants with no industrial experience – and so many were moved from job to job. The resulting high turnover in the labour market worsened the skills shortage, an already severe problem. Equipment was often used without proper training or protection, or lay idle in the new factories because no one knew how to operate or maintain it. In addition, new machinery was scarce and workers often lacked the parts needed to repair any that had been damaged.

In addition, operations were often hindered by too much interference from the party and high levels of state bureaucracy – yet, ironically, many Communist leaders such as Lenin, Trotsky and even Stalin had been critical of bureaucratisation in the past. The state's ever-expanding party apparatus and its control over the various ministries had made the system extremely inefficient, and even led to maladministration. Stalin attempted to resolve this problem by trying to increase his control over society, but in practice this just led to an increase in party officials trying to supervise each other, which only worsened this problem.

In the case of the Five-Year Plan, the party had set out its economic priorities and these were, in turn, implemented by the People's Commissariats (ministries of government departments). These local party officials worked out the targets for each region and instructions were passed down to individual factories or enterprises. Having so many levels of management meant that accountability could be, and often was, shifted from person to person. Workers were quick to blame failures on their supervisors; managers blamed the shortfall on unrealistic targets; while local officials claimed sabotage – after all, party officials could hardly blame their great leader for the confusion created by his economic policies.

As a result, when the government announced, in December 1932, that the targets of the first Five-Year Plan had officially been achieved a year early, many projects were still far from completion. The following table shows some of those production targets and compares them with the figures achieved.[12]

FIRST FIVE-YEAR PLAN, 1928–1932					
Product	1927–28 Actual	1933 target Set 1928	1932 target 1st revision	1932 target 2nd revision	1932 Actual
Coal (million tons)	**35.0**	75.0	95.0	105.0	**64.3**
Oil (million tons)	**11.7**	21.7	40.0	55.0	**21.4**
Iron ore (million tons)	**6.7**	20.2	24.0	32.0	**12.1**
Pig iron (million tons)	**3.2**	10.0	15.0	16.0	**6.2**

By 1932, urban areas and the workers in them were badly affected by food shortages. Collectivisation was making things worse, not better; towns had grown too quickly; and between 1928 and 1932, wages had been halved. So, in order to make the first Five-Year Plan appear successful, Soviet propaganda made use of new cities, such as Magnitogorsk. The limited success the plan did enjoy was due, in part, to the suffering and grit of workers, and to the elimination of those who opposed Stalin's policies. Yet in January 1933, Stalin boasted:

> We have not only created these new great industries, but have created them on a scale and in dimensions that eclipse the scale and dimensions of European industry.[13]

CONSOLIDATE YOUR KNOWLEDGE

8. Why did Stalin claim, in 1932, that the first Five-Year Plan had been a great success?

9. What did Stalin hope to achieve, politically, by implementing the first Five-Year Plan?

CONSOLIDATE YOUR KNOWLEDGE

10. In what ways did party officials help the Soviet Union work towards achieving the aims of the first Five-Year Plan?
11. From what group was most of the new industrial workforce drawn?
12. How did bureaucracy hinder the implementation of the first Five-Year Plan?
13. What other problems did the first Five-Year Plan face?
14. In economic terms, was the first Five-Year Plan a success or failure by 1932?

The party and the first Five-Year Plan

In trying to create a state controlled economy, the first Five-Year Plan is viewed by some historians as 'a revolution from above'[14] – a massive level of economic and social change imposed upon the people despite widespread opposition. While Stalin and the party championed the Five-Year Plan, many ordinary rank-and-file party members had already been pushing for the introduction of a large-scale industrialisation programme in the USSR. They wanted to remove any surviving class enemies who had not yet been eliminated or neutralised – such as kulaks, NEPmen and 'bourgeois experts' (technical experts from middle-class backgrounds) – and rapid industrialisation under the Five-Year Plans would, in theory, help to create the socialist economy promised under 'Socialism in One Country'. By dealing with the last remnants of capitalism, Stalin could win the support of hard-line, working-class party members and thus secure victory in the party's internal power struggle [see p.128].

The first Five-Year Plan was often implemented or directed by local party officials who, in many cases, owed their positions to Stalin's system of patronage. They were sometimes a little too enthusiastic and imposed party policy ruthlessly. Their zeal prompted Stalin's 'Dizzy With Success' speech in 1930, although his attempts to blame some of the failings of central planning and collectivisation on that alone were somewhat disingenuous.[15]

However, one thing was not in doubt: through implementation of most of the first Five-Year Plan, Stalin had greatly strengthened his control over both the party and the country.

CONSOLIDATE YOUR KNOWLEDGE

15. Why is the first Five-Year Plan considered a 'revolution from above'?
16. What were the ideological aims of the Five-Year Plans?
17. How did Stalin use the first Five-Year Plan to strengthen his control over the party by 1932?

The second Five-Year Plan, 1933–37

Throughout the first Five-Year Plan, the state invested in large-scale construction projects and mining. The second Five-Year Plan aimed to make greater use of the new industrial areas and technical expertise that the first plan had supposedly created. This would, in theory, consolidate the economic gains of the first plan and promoting better living standards for the new industrial workforce. It placed a greater emphasis on the development of heavy industry and the production of armaments (which trebled under the plan), aiming to make the USSR a stronger industrial state that would be more economically self-sufficient – especially in light of the growing threat posed by the Western powers.

By 1937, the second Five-Year Plan had moved on from the idea of 'industrial areas' to that of 'industrial centres'. Historian Sheila Fitzpatrick coined the term "gigantomania" in relation to these colossal industrial endeavours.[16] The second plan also aimed to improve communications between industrial areas and, to that end, chemical industries and the mining and processing of zinc, copper and tin were also developed. However, in practice at least, quantity always seemed to be more important than quality when it came to products.

When the second Five-Year Plan was launched in January 1933, large parts of the USSR (such as the cereal-producing areas of the Ukraine) were badly affected by famine. That led to continuing problems with food supplies for workers and shortages of materials for industry. There was a real struggle to obtain adequate supplies of raw materials, which were necessary for industries to reach their targets. Different sectors of industry and whole regions of the USSR ended up competing for supplies of materials, which in turn disrupted industrial production. The situation became so bad at times that some factories hoarded materials. This increased factory running costs and transport costs, and placed further strain on the suppliers of raw materials. There was a general lack of cooperation and even some corruption. Many of the goods produced were of a poor standard but this was also the time of the Great Purge [covered in section 3.4] so party officials were extremely reluctant to admit that their system had weaknesses or to criticise the second plan in any way. The plan had also been starved of funding and resources because defence spending had been increased from 4 per cent (of the total government budget) to 17 per cent by 1937.

Propaganda was used to extol the benefits of the second Five-Year Plan, at a time when the capitalist west was going through the Great Depression. The Communist Party controlled the press, cinema and radio, and they used the media to great effect [see p.132]. The best-known example of propaganda for the Five-Year Plans was the 'Stakhanovite Movement', which began in 1935. According to Soviet propaganda, a coal miner in the eastern part of the Ukraine called Alexei Stakhanov had produced, in one five-hour shift, fourteen times his usual quota of coal. Soviet workers were encouraged and inspired to follow his example and boost their production figures – those who showed particular diligence and commitment to hard work were labelled 'Stakhanovites', and in some factories they made up about one third of the workforce. On the other hand, those who failed to improve production figures could be denounced – sometimes even by their fellow workers – and some would even become victims of terror under the purges.

By 1937, the second Five-Year Plan had ended. Some lessons had been learnt from the inefficient implementation and unrealistic expectations of the first Five-Year Plan – and the state was able to make use of the industrial plants already created – so the second plan was, to some extent, more successful. Certainly, it had achieved some of its targets: workers' wages had improved a little; the USSR was now self-sufficient in metal working and machine making; and food shortages had decreased. Some historians have even called the period 1934 to 1936 the "three good years" but, as Fitzpatrick points out, "this is not saying much given that what immediately preceded these years was famine and industrial crisis".[17]

However, in many areas the second plan had failed: in 1937 living standards were still worse than they had been in 1928; and while coal production had increased substantially and there was some progress in the new chemical industry, oil-production figures showed little improvement by 1937, as shown in the table.[18]

SECOND FIVE-YEAR PLAN, 1933–1937					
Product	1927 *Actual*	1932 *Actual*	1932 *Target*	1937 *Actual*	1937 *Target*
Woollen cloth (million metres)	**97**	**93.3**	270	**108.3**	226.6
Coal (million tons)	**35.4**	**64.3**	75	**128**	152.5
Oil (million tons)	**11.7**	**21.4**	22	**28.5**	46.8
Pig iron (million tons)	**3.3**	**6.2**	10	**14.5**	16
Steel (million tons)	4	**5.9**	10.4	**17.7**	17

CONSOLIDATE YOUR KNOWLEDGE

18. Why did the second Five-Year Plan place focus more on the development of heavy industries?
19. In January 1933, what economic problems were many parts of the USSR facing?
20. How did these economic problems affect the second Five-Year Plan?
21. What were the economic weaknesses of the second Five-Year Plan?
22. Why were party officials afraid to challenge those weaknesses?
23. How did Soviet propaganda support the aims of the second Five-Year Plan?
24. In economic terms, was the second Five-Year Plan a success or a failure by 1937?

The third Five-Year Plan, 1938–41

By 1938, with the Nazi threat in Europe growing stronger, Stalin shifted his attention towards, firstly, the demands of heavy industry – with ambitious targets, such as a 58 per cent increase in steel output and a 92 per cent increase in industrial output – and secondly, the creation of a war economy. Arms production was given top priority and the whole Soviet economy was based upon creating the materials needed to build this war economy.

On 23 August 1939, a matter of days before the outbreak of the Second World War, Germany and the Soviet Union signed the Nazi-Soviet Non-Aggression Pact in which the two countries agreed they would not attack each other. This gave the USSR time to prepare for war – which they would enter in 1941.

By 1940, the defence budget was 33 per cent of the total industrial budget, while a government decree in the same year introduced even tighter controls over the labour market and workers' rights – for most workers, living standards were still lower than they had been in 1928.

The Nazi invasion of June 1941 (Operation Barbarossa) dramatically halted the implementation of the third Five-Year Plan, meaning many targets were not met. Some industries had done well – machinery and engineering (including arms) had reached 59 per cent of its planned total after three years – while others did not – the steel industry reached only 5.8 per cent of its planned target – but it can be argued that the third Five-Year plan had better prepared the Soviet economy for events in Europe, and ultimately enabled the USSR to fight and win the Second World War.

CONSOLIDATE YOUR KNOWLEDGE

25. What were the main aims of the third Five-Year Plan?
26. Why was this plan brought to a sudden end in 1941?

GROUP ACTIVITY

Organise a class debate with the motion:

"The Five-Year Plans were an economic success for Stalin by 1941."

TASK

Copy out the table below and summarise the main features and aims of each of the three Five-Year Plans between 1928 and 1941.

Five-Year Plan	Features and aims
First plan: 1928–32	
Second plan: 1933–37	
Third plan: 1938–41	

The effects of the Five-Year Plans by 1941

Industrialisation and the Five-Year Plans had impacted on many things by 1941, but the economic, social and political effects are particularly relevant:

Economic

- There was a focus on heavy industry, which is vital for a war economy.
- Large, new industrial centres (i.e. industrial estates and surrounding new towns) were laid out.
- Huge factories were constructed.
- Centralised planning and control of industry were poor. The efficiency of factories was reduced.
- There were shortages of some key materials needed for industry.
- The quality of goods produced was often poor.
- Steel production rose by 400 per cent.
- Coal production rose by 600 per cent.
- The production (and therefore availability) of consumer goods declined.
- Most important areas of the USSR were connected to the electricity grid.

Social

- Peasants were forced to leave their land.
- Millions of peasants moved to urban areas.

- Millions of women became industrial workers.
- There was no major improvement in living conditions.
- In general, wages and working conditions declined.
- Passports were introduced for travel within the USSR, in order to control workers.
- Political prisoners were used to fill gaps in the labour supply.
- Collectivisation led to food shortages and famine.
- Any unrest in factories was dealt with by force or the threat of force.
- There was a significant loss of life.

Political

- Capitalists, the bourgeoisie (middle classes) and kulaks (better-off peasants) ceased to exist as classes.
- NEPmen and bourgeois technical experts lost positions and/or influence.
- Stalin was able to remove the Right Opposition.
- Through Gosplan, the state increased its control over the economy.
- The role of government was greatly expanded.
- The state gained more control over industrial workers.
- Propaganda was used to explain the Five-Year Plans to the people of the USSR.
- Stalin's personal grip on power was strengthened.

By 1941, the three Five-Year Plans appeared to have transformed the USSR from a backward agrarian society into a modern industrial state – this was an economic revolution with enormous social and political consequences [covered in section 4.4].

Conclusions

The Five-Year Plans had been implemented and fought like a class war against the NEPmen and kulaks. However, the removal of the NEPmen and bourgeois technical experts during the first Five-Year Plan slowed the rate of progress under the two subsequent plans – these technical experts were replaced with party officials who often lacked the skills of their predecessors. Similarly, unskilled peasants were unable to use some of the new technology that the Five-Year Plans provided.

The focus on the production of raw materials and competition for those materials – encouraged by unrealistic targets – led to further inefficiencies and personal rivalries that dented the statistics even more. Yet, even though the human cost was high, there is no denying that the USSR made significant industrial advances by 1941. As Sheila Fitzpatrick surmises, modern technology "was essential to the process of catching up and surpassing … Factories were built for assembly-line production … backward Russia would soon become Soviet America."[19]

Certainly Stalin's pride in the advances of industry cannot be denied. As he boasted in November 1929, during his speech at the 16th Party Congress, "We are becoming a country of metal, a country of automobiles, a country of tractors."[20]

CONSOLIDATE YOUR KNOWLEDGE

27. To what extent had the Five-Year Plans achieved their economic aims by 1941?

28. Why had the Five-Year Plans failed to achieve many of their economic aims by 1941?

29. Were the Five-Year Plans an economic success or failure by 1941?

30. Why was there opposition to collectivisation and the Five-Year Plans?

4.4: The Social Impact of Stalin's Economic Policies, 1928–41

Between 1928 and 1941, Stalin created Socialism in One Country, mainly through collectivisation and the implementation of the Five-Year Plans. The country was transformed into a modern industrial economy, and Soviet propaganda boasted of great economic achievements. Incentives were introduced to encourage workers and peasants to meet the set production targets but, ultimately, citizens of the USSR paid a terrible price for the country's transformation, and that price was completely ignored by the state.

The system depended on the use of terror, and millions of people lost their lives. Those who failed to meet targets were punished and absenteeism became a capital offence. Workers could not change jobs without the permission of a government agency. Movement within the USSR was controlled by internal passports. Workers' lives and even their leisure time were controlled by legislation. Opposition to the Stalinist system was often dealt with by execution or by the Gulag system. For the vast majority of Soviet citizens, living and working conditions remained poor. Housing was overcrowded and shoddy. Food shortages were widespread, and the dearth of consumer goods in shops often led to bribery and under-the-counter deals.

Industry suffered from shortages of skilled labour. Agriculture struggled because of the effects of collectivisation. Disgruntled peasants might eventually have been appeased, to an extent, by the provision of private plots but Stalin's 'economic planning' was, in reality, a form of social engineering designed to meet his political objectives. His economic policies meant that, by 1941, the lives of all Soviet citizens were controlled by the state. The social impact of these changes was felt across the USSR.

CONSOLIDATE YOUR KNOWLEDGE

1. How were workers encouraged to meet the economic targets set by the government?
2. Describe two social problems facing Soviet citizens in the 1930s.
3. How were Stalin's economic policies being used as a means of social control over the people of the USSR by 1941?

The role of women

Three new sources of labour provided the bulk of the new industrial workforce. Firstly, millions of peasants moved from their rural homes to the new towns and cities, which were built around factories. Secondly, political prisoners – the number of which had greatly increased – were sent to the Gulag camps in the 1930s. Thirdly, women were encouraged to take up jobs.

Government policies still encouraged women to have large families, but the party also emphasised their increased importance to the Soviet labour force. Encouraged by this, some women in urban areas joined special female construction brigades. In agriculture, collectivisation grew ever more reliant on female labour, although it was economic necessity, rather than Stalinist propaganda, that often forced women into paid employment – in rural areas, for instance, many men had deserted their families and gone to find manufacturing jobs in new towns.

By the early 1930s, more than 40 per cent of all new workers were female. They tended to be younger and more inexperienced than their male counterparts, but they held a greater range of jobs than women in most Western societies at the time. By the end of the 1930s women occupied 70 per cent of the positions in the textile industry, and 24 per cent of those in mining and engineering. By 1940, over thirteen million industrial workers were women, compared with about three million in 1928.

In 1929, women had been under-represented within the party bureaucracy and in higher education, but the new expanded education and healthcare systems were increasingly attractive and, by 1940, over 40 per cent of engineering students were female (compared to just under 20 per cent in 1929).

CONSOLIDATE YOUR KNOWLEDGE

4. How did the economic role of women change between 1928 and 1941?

5. Why were women encouraged to take up jobs after 1928?

6. In which sectors of the economy were women especially important by 1941?

Migration and the growth of the urban population

During the period between 1928 and 1941, migration to the USSR's urban areas had profound social consequences – some of the effects were positive but many were negative. Urban unemployment was eradicated as mass industrialisation created millions of jobs, and in the early years of the first Five-Year Plan, the urban population was growing by about 200,000 people per month – a total growth of about 30 million people between 1926 and 1930.

There was a huge population shift: industrial cities and areas, particularly new ones, grew but the agricultural workforce fell by 13 million (from 61 million in 1928, to 48 million people in 1939). When the young and educated headed off to urban areas, the rural areas they left behind tended to become more conservative (one reason why religion still had its place in the countryside), however life in rapidly expanding urban areas was far from easy for the new, young labour force.

Many of the new cities were little more than very large building sites. People lived in dirt and squalor. In Magnitogorsk, for example, 25 per cent of workers lived in huts they had made themselves. Only 15 per cent lived in conventionally constructed apartment blocks. Most workers found that, at some stage, they had to live in vast complexes, which were laid out like army barracks or camps. Conditions were often terrible. In some remote areas, new towns lacked paved roads and proper drainage. In fact, the worst examples were, in reality, just like shanty towns, in which crime and violence were common.

A poster for the 17th Congress of the Communist Party, showing Lenin, Stalin and the new Russia, 1934.

Housing was overcrowded, and sanitisation standards were very low, with little or no privacy. Women suffered most from situations such as these. In 1930, the average Moscow resident had a mere 5.5m^2 of living space. By 1940, that figure had dropped to just 4m^2 of living space, per person. By the 1930s, there was a noticeable difference between the conditions endured by the urban poor and those enjoyed by party officials and managers.

Far from solving the problems of food production and distribution, collectivisation led to severe food shortages in the new urban areas. Queues were an everyday feature of Soviet life and food rationing was not unknown. In Moscow and Leningrad, meat, milk and fruit consumption declined by 66 per cent between 1928 and 1933. There were hardly any cafes or restaurants and, in some cases, even drinking water was in short supply. In the 1930s there were few shops and stocks of consumer goods were low. Very limited ranges were available and most of the items that could be bought were of poor quality. Many had to be supplied through the burgeoning black market.

CONSOLIDATE YOUR KNOWLEDGE

7. Why did the urban population of the USSR grow so quickly between 1928 and 1941?
8. Why did the rural population decline by 1941?
9. Describe the main problems that faced the new urban population.
10. Why were Soviet workers' living conditions so poor in the 1930s?

Opposition and terror

In some rural areas there had been fierce resistance to collectivisation but, as Stalin had already demonstrated, his regime did not tolerate opposition of any kind – least of all to collectivisation or the Five-Year Plans.

An early example of Stalin's crackdown on 'class enemies' was the Shakhty Trial of 1928: a show trial of several mining engineers from the Russian part of the Caucasus who were accused of industrial sabotage and of collaborating with the (exiled) former owners of the coal mines. Then in 1930, engineers in the Donbas region of eastern Ukraine were arrested and several scientists were shot. In 1933, there was a trial of some British electrical engineers from the Metropolitan-Vickers company, accused of economic 'wrecking' and espionage.

State terror was used to make citizens accept state control of all aspects of the economy and of all aspects of their lives. Between 1934 and 1939, millions of people were accused of being hostile towards Stalin's economic policies. Even those supportive of the programmes were not spared – some were denounced for failing to reach the unrealistic targets set by the Five-Year Plans. People were either executed as part of his purges or arrested and sent to Gulag camps.

The first labour camps had been established in 1929. In 1930, there were six camps and some Western historians claim that, by 1931, at least two million people were imprisoned in Gulags – though there are no accurate records for this period. What is known is that these political prisoners were being used as a source of labour. They were hired out by the secret police, which had arranged the building of roads and canals often in the most remote regions of the USSR, such as Siberia, where many Gulag camps were located. Raw materials, such as diamonds, gold, platinum, nickel, oil, coal and timber, were often found in such places – the secret police even organised their own gold rush in Siberia – and the Gulags enabled the exploitation of very remote regions for the first time. Working conditions were atrocious but the authorities showed no mercy. The regime and its agencies regarded prisoners' lives as expendable.

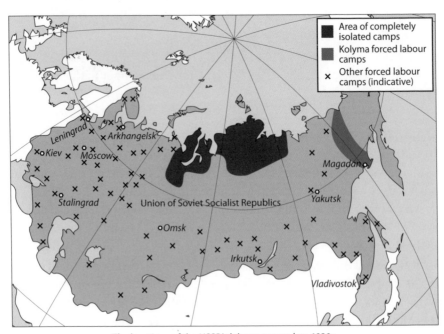

The locations of the USSR's labour camps, late 1930s.

By the 1930s, in a desperate attempt to meet the targets of the Five-Year Plans, millions of political prisoners were being used as slave labour.Huge infrastructure projects (such as the Moscow Metro, the city of Magnitogorsk and new canals) were built by Gulag prisoners. These political prisoners were also forced to build the Belomor Canal (linking the Baltic to the White Sea) at the cost of hundreds of thousands of lives. Sadly, despite the heavy sacrifices made, it was something of a white elephant: it was opened in 1933 and, although Soviet propaganda made great use of its completion, it was of limited transport value in real terms. As historian Orlando Figes puts it:

> Built on top of bones, the canal was a fitting symbol of the Stalinist regime, whose greatest propaganda successes were achieved with a total disregard for the millions of lives they cost.[21]

Gulag prisoners forced to work on the Belomor Canal, 1931.

The economic progress made during the 1930s was built upon the deaths and injuries of Gulag victims and the secret police became one of the driving forces behind Soviet industrialisation. By 1941, the millions of political prisoners had created railways, canals and mines. The Great Terror had become an integral part of the Soviet economic system and, although the mass-murder machine was wound down at the very end of the 1930s, political prisoners continued to play a very important role in the economy for some years after Stalin's death in 1953. Stalin wanted economic development at any price but millions of innocent Soviet citizens bore the brunt of his policies.

CONSOLIDATE YOUR KNOWLEDGE

11. Explain the role of the Gulag organisation and its camps within the Soviet economy.

12. What was the human cost of using the Gulags to turn the USSR into an industrial power?

13. In which parts of the USSR was forced labour used? Why was it used?

14. What was the most important social impact of Stalin's policies by 1941?

GROUP ACTIVITY

As a group, and using your own knowledge and research, explain the social impact that Stalin's economic policies would have had on the people of the Soviet Union by 1941.

Discuss and present your findings.

Revision Section: Stalin's Economic Policies, 1924–41

This section will give a summary of the main events and developments in relation to Stalin and the Soviet economy from1924, leading up to the Nazi invasion of Russia in 1941. Students must appreciate the impact of each stage on the USSR and its people and understand the most important of Stalin's policies. To help students prepare for assessments and unit tests there will be some brief summaries of these key events – which should underline their importance and help to consolidate knowledge – along with a few sample exam questions.

Independent research, looking at key figures and events, will help you develop a deeper understanding of Stalin's economic-policy objectives and the way he tried to reach them.

Turning point 1: Stalin and collectivisation, 1928–41

There is a need to understand the main features and aims of collectivisation in the years between 1928 and 1941. Collectivisation had a significant impact on the USSR.

Successes
- 97 per cent of all Soviet farms were collectivised.
- Millions of peasants were moved from the countryside.
- Soviet agriculture was mechanised.
- Collective farms (singular *kolkhoz*, plural *kolkhozy*) had been established and were much larger than traditional peasant farms.
- There were limited increases in food production.
- Agriculture and peasants were brought under state control.
- It was a useful propaganda tool (both internally and externally) for the Soviet regime.
- The opposition of peasants to collectivisation had been crushed.
- Collectivisation seemed to complement the Five-Year Plans.
- The kulaks and NEPmen were destroyed, as social and political groups.

Failures

- The human cost was huge with millions of lives lost.
- Food shortages and famine were widespread.
- Agricultural skills were lost after the destruction of the kulaks as a class.
- Officials, put in charge of collective farms, often knew little about farming. Agriculture therefore suffered.
- Agricultural production in 1939 remained lower than it had been in 1913.
- Improvements in agriculture were limited or non-existent.
- Peasants remained uncooperative, making such improvements harder.
- Some peasants who opposed collectivisation destroyed their own farm buildings, livestock and crops.
- The principal areas of agriculture e.g. Ukraine) were badly affected.
- Soviet agriculture was still unable to feed industrial workers.
- From 1931 onwards, Stalin was forced to allow peasants to have their own small plots in order to appease them.
- Agriculture was not prepared for war in 1941.
- The living standards of peasants were no better in 1941 than they had been in 1928.

Turning point 2: Stalin and industrialisation

There is also a need to understand the main features and aims of Stalin's policy of industrialisation and its implementation through three Five-Year Plans. The Five-Year Plan, as a concept, had very noticeable and lasting effects on the USSR.

Successes

- Gigantic industrial projects were completed.
- The USSR had a more modern and much larger industrial economy by 1941.
- New industrial cities and industrial areas had been created.
- The Soviet economy was better prepared for war in 1941 than it had been in 1938.
- Resources were obtained from areas like Siberia, which, before the 1930s, had not been exploited to a great extent.
- The apparent success of the Five-Year Plans could be contrasted (in Soviet propaganda) with the Great Depression in Western countries.

- Electricity became more widely available for the people and industry.
- The Soviet government gained greater control over industry and the workers.
- Some new industries (such as the chemical industry) were developed.
- There was greater mechanisation – use of assembly-line techniques and so on – in Soviet factories.
- There were noticeable increases in production, particularly for coal and steel.

Failures
- The Five-Year Plans had a terrible human cost – millions lost their lives.
- Many targets were not met, partly because of state bureaucracy.
- Shortages of consumer goods continued.
- Skills shortages also continued.
- The Gulag (labour-camp organisation) had to assist with the construction of large projects.
- Some projects were of very limited economic or social value, such as the Belomor Canal.
- Implementation of the third Five-Year Plan was made difficult because defence spending distorted the Soviet economy.
- The conditions in which workers lived did not really improve between 1928 and 1941.
- Conditions in the factories and in workers' homes took a heavy toll on their health and personal lives.
- New technology and machines proved to be unreliable.
- The Five-Year Plans' chances of success were damaged by Stalin's purges.
- The breakneck pace of change damaged the economy.
- Much of what was produced was of poor quality.
- Production levels were not steady. Sometimes, too much was produced and, sometimes, too little.
- There had been growth in some areas of manufacturing, but the transformation was not as impressive as it might have been.

PRACTICE EXAMINATION QUESTIONS, 1924–41

Based on format of questions for CCEA Unit AS2, Option 5 (Russia).

These questions are for individual or class-based use and study. Questions from past papers and specimen papers can be accessed through the CCEA GCE History microsite.

www.rewardinglearning.org.uk/microsites/history/gce/past_papers/index.asp

These are some sample 8-mark and 22-mark examination-type questions, to help students to prepare and practice for assessment tasks for this period.

8-mark questions (short responses)

a) Explain why Stalin allowed the NEP to continue between 1924 and 1928.

b) Explain Stalin's economic aims when he introduced collectivisation after 1928.

c) Explain the main features of collectivisation.

d) Explain the economic aims of Stalin's first Five-Year Plan.

e) Explain the main features of the first Five-Year Plan.

f) Explain the effects of Stalin's economic policies on the role of women in the USSR between 1928 and 1941?

22-mark questions (essay answers)

- "By 1941, Stalin had failed to achieve his economic aims for the USSR." To what extent do you agree with this verdict on the period 1928–1941?

- How far would you agree that, between 1928 and 1941, Stalin's industrial policies were more successful than his agricultural ones?

- "Between 1928 and 1941, collectivisation achieved Stalin's economic aims for the Soviet Union but at tremendous human cost." How far would you accept this statement?

- "Stalin's economic policies lacked consistency between 1928 and 1941." How far would you agree with this judgement?

Endnotes

1   Fitzpatrick, Sheila, *The Russian Revolution* (Oxford University Press, 1994), p.131

2   Kotkin, Stephen, *Magnetic Mountain: Stalinism as a Civilization* (University of California Press, 1997) p.29

3   Welch, David, *Modern European History 1871–2000* (Routledge, 2003) p.94

4   The singular being *kolkhoz*.

5   Stalin, J.V., 'Dizzy With Success', *Pravda,* 2 March 1930

6   *From* Philips, Steve, *Stalinist Russia* (Heinemann, 2000) p.36

7   *From* Lynch, Michael, *Access to History: Russia 1894–1941*, eBook (Hodder, 2015)

8   Figes, Orlando, *Revolutionary Russia, 1891–1991*, eBook (Penguin, 2014)

9   *From* Fitzpatrick, Sheila, *The Russian Revolution* (Oxford University Press, 1994) p.131

10 *From* Figes, Orlando, *The Whisperers: Private Life in Stalin's Russia*, eBook (Penguin, 2008)

11 Service, Robert, *Comrades!: A History of World Communism* (Harvard University Press, 2007) p.183

12 *From* Nove, Alec, *An Economic History of the USSR 1917–1991* (Penguin, 1972), p.188

13 Kishlansky, Mark A., Patrick J. Geary, Patricia O'Brien, *Civilization in the West, Volume 2* (Longman, 2003), p.891

14 *For example, see* Figes, *Revolutionary Russia*

15 Stalin, 'Dizzy With Success', *Pravda*

16 Fitzpatrick, Sheila, *The Russian Revolution* (Oxford University Press, 1994) p.134

17 Fitzpatrick, Sheila, *Everyday Stalinism: Ordinary Life in Extraordinary Times: Soviet Russia in the 1930s*, eBook (Oxford University Press, 1999)

18 *From* Nove, Alec, *An Economic History of the USSR 1917–1991* (Penguin, 1972). p.188 & 225

19 Fitzpatrick, Sheila, *The Russian Revolution* (Oxford University Press, 1994) pp.134–5

20 Figes, Orlando, *Revolutionary Russia, 1891–1991*, (Penguin, 2014), p.207

21 Figes, Orlando, *Revolutionary Russia, 1891–1991*, (Penguin, 2014) p.223

Biographical Notes

Bukharin, Nikolai (1888–1938)

Bukharin emerged after the October Revolution as an important economic theorist and party intellectual. He became a loyal Lenin supporter, defending his position over Brest-Litovsk and the adoption of the NEP in 1921. After Lenin's death in 1924, Bukharin supported Stalin (mostly due to his own personal opposition to Trotsky.) Bukharin helped develop 'Socialism in One Country', which Stalin adopted as official Soviet policy. After Trotsky's political defeat by 1927, Bukharin became politically isolated and was removed from the Politburo in 1929. He was editor of *Izvestia* from 1934 to 1937. He also drafted the new Soviet Constitution of 1936. In March 1938 Bukharin became a victim of the show trials and was executed.

Kamenev, Lev Rosenfeld (1883–1936)

Born into a wealthy Moscow Jewish family, Kamenev (his revolutionary name) was a founding member of the Bolshevik Party. In the run up to October Revolution, he opposed Lenin's plans for a seizure of power to overthrow the Provisional Government. Despite this, Lenin appointed Kamenev as the first chairman of the Politburo. Kamenev was a moderate who supported party unity but was opposed to Trotsky's policies. After 1922, with Lenin's frequent absences, Kamenev formed a triumvirate with Zinoviev and Stalin to run Russia. In 1925, Kamenev lost political influence. He was removed from the Politburo, joining an anti-Stalin alliance with Zinoviev and Trotsky. Between 1925 and 1936, Kamenev was expelled and readmitted to the Communist Party (CPSU) several times. In August 1936, in the first major show trial, Kamenev was executed after claiming to have murdered Sergey Kirov.

Kerensky, Alexander (1881–1970)

Brought up in Simbirsk, Kerensky studied law and history at St Petersburg University. He joined the (moderate-socialist) Socialist Revolutionary Party in 1905 when he was a young lawyer, and eventually became leader. Elected to the Duma in December 1912, he rose to prominence as an anti-tsarist spokesman. After the February Revolution of 1917, he emerged as a leading member of the Provisional Government and was made minister of justice. In the summer of 1917, he became minister of war and then in July 1917, he became prime minister, taking up residence in the headquarters of the Provisional Government (at the Winter Palace). In August 1917, he sought Bolshevik support to stop General Lavr Kornilov with disastrous consequences. In October 1917, the Bolsheviks removed Kerensky from power, but he escaped arrest and fled into political exile in Paris. By 1940, Kerensky was living in New York, where he died in 1970.

Kirov, Sergey (1886–1934)

Kirov joined the Bolsheviks in 1904 and was a loyal supporter of Lenin and Stalin after the October Revolution. In 1926, he was appointed head of the party in Leningrad, and in 1930, he became a member of the Politburo. Kirov was a popular figure within the party and he appeared to be Stalin's potential successor. In December 1934, after winning much support at that year's Communist Party Congress, he was murdered. Stalin, who has been blamed for orchestrating Kirov's murder, used his death to justify the Great Purges that followed.

Lenin, Vladimir Ilyich Ulyanov (1870–1924)

Vladimir Ilyich Ulyanov was born in 1870 into a middle-class family of Jewish descent. In 1887, the execution of his older brother for revolutionary activity inspired him to become a radical. In 1897, he was exiled to Siberia where he adopted his revolutionary name of Lenin. In 1900, he joined the Russian Social Democratic Labour Party (RSDLP) and led the Bolsheviks after the party split in 1903. He returned to Russia during the 1905 Revolution but he played no real role. From 1906, he lived in exile abroad – mainly in Switzerland – and in April 1917, after the February Revolution, he returned to Petrograd where he led the successful Bolshevik October Revolution. He survived an assassination attempt in 1918, but it caused a steady decline in his health. His last major policy change was the introduction of the NEP in 1921. From 1922 onwards, he was effectively incapacitated and other senior Bolsheviks – the triumvirate of Zinoviev, Kamenev and Stalin – ruled Russia until his eventual death in 1924. Stalin had his body embalmed and placed on public display in Moscow.

Molotov, Vyacheslav (1890–1986)

Molotov came from a middle class family, joining the Bolsheviks after the 1905 Revolution. He was a loyal supporter of Lenin and then of Stalin. In 1925, Molotov became a member of the Politburo and in 1930, he became chairman of the Sovnarkom. In 1939, he was made commissar for foreign affairs and helped draw up the Nazi-Soviet Pact. Molotov served under Stalin until 1949 and died in Moscow in 1986.

Rasputin, Grigori (1872–1916)

There is a lack of reliable information on Rasputin's early life, but he became a self-styled Orthodox priest and mystic healer, and enjoyed contact with the royal household. Despite the scandal surrounding Rasputin, Tsarina Alexandra became dependent upon him to take care of her only son, who suffered from haemophilia. Under the treatments of this so-called 'Holy Wanderer', the health of the Tsarevich Alexei seemed to improve. Rasputin's political influence over government increased after 1915 when the tsar became commander-in-chief of the armed forces [see p.18]. Rumours of an affair with the tsarina, along with his political unpopularity, led to his murder in December 1916 by a group of Russian aristocrats trying to protect tsarism.

Rykov, Alexei (1881–1938)

Rykov joined the Bolsheviks in 1905. He was a loyal supporter of Lenin but was opposed to the plans to seize power in October 1917. After the October Revolution, Rykov was appointed commissar for internal affairs – a post he held until 1924 – and made head of the Vesenkha (the Supreme Council of the National Economy). Rykov was also Lenin's deputy on the Sovnarkom. After Lenin's death, Rykov supported Stalin against Trotsky, siding with Tomsky and Bukharin. Rykov was a leading member of the Right Opposition before his removal from political power. In 1930, Rykon was removed from all party posts and expelled from the Politburo. In March 1938, he became another victim of the show trials, which led to his execution.

Stalin, Joseph Dzhughashvili (1879–1953)

Stalin was born into a working-class family in Georgia. In 1901, he joined the RSDLP and supported Lenin after the 1903 party split. After many spells in prison he became the first leading Bolshevik to return to Petrograd after the February Revolution. He became more politically important after the 1917 October Revolution and, in 1922, he became general secretary of the Communist Party. In 1929, he eventually won the power struggle taking place since Lenin's death in 1924, and he set about creating a dictatorship in the USSR. In 1928, he launched the first of a series of Five-Year Plans that, along with collectivisation, modernised the Soviet Union's economy. After 1934, he launched a series of purges that continued until Germany's invasion of the USSR in 1941. By 1945, Stalin had won the Second World War, and by 1948, the USSR controlled most of Eastern Europe. In 1949, Stalin was forced to back down over the Berlin Blockade. He died in March 1953.

Tomsky, Mikhail (1880–1936)

Tomsky was the only leading Bolshevik in 1917, apart from Stalin, to come from a working-class background. After the October Revolution he represented the trade union movement and the interests of the workers within the party. In 1920, he became head of the trade union movement, and in 1922, he was appointed to the Politburo. Tomsky was a strong supporter of Bukharin and, along with Bukharin and Rykov, became a leading member of the Right. In 1930, he was removed from the Politburo. In August 1936, during the first major show trials in Moscow, Tomsky committed suicide to avoid arrest and execution.

Trotsky, Leon (1879–1940)

Born Lev Bronshteinorn in 1879 to a wealthy Ukrainian Jewish family, he was convicted of revolutionary activities in 1898, and in 1902, adopted the name Trotsky. In 1903, after the RSDLP party split, he became a Menshevik and, during the 1905 Revolution, he became chairman of the St Petersburg Soviet. From 1907, Trotsky lived in exile abroad, and was in New York at the time of the 1917 February Revolution. In the summer of 1917, Trotsky returned to Russia and converted to Bolshevism. He set up the Military Revolutionary Committee (MRC) and played a major role in organising and planning the October Revolution. In 1918, he was in charge of foreign affairs and negotiated the Treaty of Brest-Litovsk. He created the Red Army and led the campaign for the Reds in the civil war, crushing the Kronstadt Rebellion in 1921. After Lenin's death in 1924, Trotsky lost political influence and authority. In 1927, he was placed in internal exile, and in 1929, he was banished from the USSR. Trotsky openly criticised Stalin and his regime throughout the 1930s, and while in Mexico in 1940, was murdered by a Soviet agent.

Tsar Nicholas II (1868–1918)

Nicholas was tsar of Russia from 1894 until his abdication in 1917. In 1905, he granted the *The Manifesto on the Improvement of the State Order* ('October Manifesto'), which served as a precursor to Russia's first constitution, and in 1906, he opened the first Russian Imperial State Duma (parliament). In 1913, he and his family celebrated three hundred years of Romanov rule in Russia. In 1914, he approved instructions that led to Russia joining the First World War in alliance with France and Britain. In 1915, he appointed himself commander-in-chief of the Russian army. By early 1917, as problems worsened in Petrograd, he tried to return to the capital but was forced to abdicate. By the end of 1917, the tsar and his family were prisoners of the Bolsheviks, and in July 1918, they were murdered on Lenin's orders.

Tsarina Alexandra (1872–1918)

Born 1872, a German princess and a granddaughter of Queen Victoria, she married Tsar Nicholas II in 1894. Together they had four daughters and one son, the Tsarevich Alexei who was heir to the Russian throne. From 1915 onwards, with the tsar leading the armed forces, the tsarina became more politically important. However she grew dependent upon advice from Rasputin, becoming politically isolated and unpopular between 1915 and 1917. Forced to abdicate in February 1917, she was murdered by the Bolsheviks in July 1918, along with the tsar and their five children.

Zinoviev, Gregory (1883–1936)

From 1908, Zinoviev, an active member of the Bolsheviks, spent most of his time in political exile working closely with Lenin. After the failure of the July Days, the two men then fled to exile in Finland. Along with Kamenev, Zinoviev opposed Lenin's plans for a seizure of power in October 1917, yet after the October Revolution he was a founder member of the first Politburo. In 1919, he was appointed as the first chairman of the Comintern. Due to Lenin's growing ill health, Zinoviev, Kamenev and Stalin formed a triumvirate to govern the USSR, which continued after Lenin's death in 1924. After being politically isolated by Stalin, Zinoviev forged a political alliance with Kamenev and Trotsky. In 1926, Zinoviev lost his place on the Comintern and the Politburo, and in 1927 he was expelled from the CPSU for the first time. He was executed in August 1936 after his show trial.

Glossary

This is a list of key words and terms used throughout the book.

Agitprop: The political propaganda used by the USSR to spread their message to citizens through all forms of mass media.

April Theses: The new set of political ideas that Lenin issued just after his return to Russia in April 1917.

Atheism: A lack of religious beliefs. The Communist regime encouraged this as it undermined the power of the churches.

Bolsheviks: Following the RSDLP party split of 1903, they supported Lenin and believed that they had to lead a revolution in Russia. Their name comes from the Russian word for majority.

Bourgeois experts: Former middle-class or well-educated experts, especially in the Stalin period of economic change.

Bureaucratisation: The structure of control over the Soviet Union created by the Communist regime. The level of bureaucracy the state created actually made it inefficient.

Central Committee: The decision making body of the Bolshevik party. In March 1919 it became the Politburo.

Cheka: The secret police Lenin created in December 1917. In 1922 it became the OGPU.

Collectivisation: Stalin's policy to modernise Soviet agriculture – the state created massive collective farms across the USSR, mainly during the 1930s.

Comintern: Also known as the Communist International, this was the body Lenin set up in March 1919 to encourage and promote a worldwide revolution. It was dissolved in 1943.

Commissariat for Education: Also known as Narkompos, this body was in charge of education and schools and ensured conformity with Communist ideology and culture. It was formed in 1918.

Communism: The ideology that adhered to Marxist philosophy and meant support for the USSR.

Constituent Assembly: This was to be a new, all-Russian democratic parliament. Elected in late 1917, it was dissolved by the Bolsheviks after only one day in January 1918.

Constructivists: A group of artists led by Vladimir Tatlin, who had new ideas for arts and architecture under the Communist regime.

CPSU: The new name given to the Bolsheviks in March 1918 – better known as the Communist Party.

Cultural revolution: Lenin believed that the Communist party had to lead a major cultural change amongst the citizens of the USSR. This policy continued under Stalin into the early 1930s.

Dual Authority: Also known as Dual Power, this refers to the political set up in 1917 when, thanks to Soviet Order Number 1, both the Provisional Government and the Soviets appeared to share power in Russia.

Duma: The Russian parliament. Set up by the tsar, there were four in total between 1906 and 1917.

Factionalism: Organised opposition within the Communist Party. In March 1921, Lenin introduced a party ban on factionalism.

Fellow travellers: Artists and writers within the USSR who did not actively support the new Communist state but went along with its ideas. The term was first used by Trotsky in 1925.

Five-Year Plans: A series of state led plans to spread industrialisation across the Soviet Union from 1928 to 1941.

Foreign intervention: The use of armies sent by the Western powers to help the Whites against the Reds during the Civil War in Russia.

Futurists: A group of Russian poets and artists who wanted radical cultural changes and believed in modernisation under the Communist regime.

Gosizdat: The body that, in May 1919, became Russia's state publishing house. It was replaced in 1930 by OGIZ (United State Publishing House).

Gosplan: The body set up in February 1921 to draw up an economic plan for all of Russia. It became more important in the 1930s because of its role in the Five-Year Plans.

Grain requisitioning: The policy forced upon the peasantry during War Communism to meet economic production targets set by the Bolshevik regime.

Gulags: The forced labour camps built in the remote regions of the USSR, which rapidly increased on a large scale during the 1930s. Many victims of the purges were sent to the Gulags, where they would work on massive labour projects.

Izvestiya: ('The News') The Bolshevik newspaper published for the first time in February 1917.

Kadets: Also known as the Constitutional Democrats, a liberal political party formed after the 1905 Revolution – they wanted Russia to become a constitutional monarchy.

Kolskhozy: The large, state-owned farms created as part of collectivisation.

Komsomol: The Communist Union of Youth that had different sections for young people of different ages. It was originally formed in 1918 and was restructured in the 1920s.

Kulaks: The better-off farmers who had benefitted from Stolypin's land reforms and the NEP Under Stalin they were portrayed as a reactionary class who were to be eliminated in the 1930s.

League of Militant Atheists: Formed in 1925, this was a body set up to encourage Soviet citizens to reject all forms of organised religion.

Lenin Enrolment: A period between 1923 and 1925 when Communist Party membership numbers increased rapidly (from about 300,000 to 600,000 people).

Leninism: Lenin's interpretation of Marxism between 1917 and 1924. It is also known as Marxism-Leninism.

Marxism: The ideals of Karl Marx and his followers, who are often known as Communists.

Mensheviks: The group who rejected Lenin's ideas during the RSDLP party split of 1903 as they believed in an inevitable revolution. Their name comes from the Russian word for minority.

Military Revolutionary Committee (MRC): Led by Trotsky, this was set up to organise and plan the Bolshevik seizure of power in October 1917 by the soviets.

Nationalities issue: Many parts of Russia (such as the Ukraine and Georgia in particular) had a strong regional national identity that both the tsarist regime and the Communist regime felt had to be suppressed.

NEPmen: Those who did well under the NEP, such as small traders and businessmen in particular, by 1924.

New Economic Policy (NEP): The economic policy implemented by Lenin in March 1921 to allow the Russian economy to recover, particularly given the recent civil war.

New Style (NS): A way to denote dates in the Gregorian calendar, which Russia adopted in February 1918.

NKVD: The USSR's state secret police from 1934 onwards.

OGPU: The state secret police from 1922 to 1934.

Okhrana: The Russian secret police under the tsar. Abolished after the February Revolution of 1917.

Old Style (OS): A way to denote dates in the Julian calendar, which Russia used until February 1918.

Orgburo: Short for organisational bureau, this body was set up in early 1919 to focus on the problem of party organisation and to turn Communist policies into practice.

Party Congress: The national party meetings of the Communist Party in Russia – it was the supreme body of the party.

Permanent Revolution: The theory Trotsky developed between 1906 and 1917 – it believed in a continued process of international class warfare.

Personality cult: A process in which a country's regime creates an idealised and often worshipful image of a leader. Under Stalin an overwhelming cult of personality grew around the Great Leader.

Politburo: The executive decision-making body of the CPSU that replaced the Central Committee in March 1919.

Pravda: Meaning 'the Truth', this was the official Bolshevik newspaper, published by the Central Committee of the CPSU.

Proletariat: The Marxist term for the exploited industrial working classes who formed the vast majority of the Russian population in 1917.

Progressive Bloc: In June 25 1915, 236 out of 422 Duma members formed this group to support the tsar but it later became a source of political resistance to the tsarist regime.

Proletkult: An abbreviation of 'proletarian culture', a cultural revolutionary movement that emerged just before the October Revolution. It became a mass movement under Lenin until it was brought under the control of the Commissariat of Education in December 1920.

Propaganda: The range of materials produced by the Communist regime to portray the benefits of Communism to Soviet citizens.

Provisional Government: The new Russian Government that emerged following the February Revolution – formed from members of the Duma.

Purges: The widespread policies of repression carried out by the secret police under Stalin's orders in the 1930s.

RAPP: The Russian Association of Proletarian Writers. It was very influential between 1928 and 1931 but was dissolved in April 1932.

Red Terror: The ruthless policies implemented by the Bolsheviks to enforce War Communism upon the people of Russia.

Right Opposition: Members of the CPSU who opposed Stalin's policies of rapid industrialisation and the end of the NEP They were defeated and removed from influential party positions by 1929–30.

Romanovs: The Russian royal family who had ruled as an autocracy since 1613.

RSDLP: The Russian Social and Democratic Workers Party. Inspired by the work of Marx and Engels, the party was formed in 1898, but in 1903 split into two factions – the Bolsheviks and the Mensheviks.

Secretariat: The body that carried out the administration of government policies under the Soviet regime.

Show trials: A series of trials of Old Bolshevik leaders as part of the 1930s purges.

Socialism in One Country: An overall term for the radical new economic policies Stalin introduced to create a modern socialist state in the USSR that could stand up to Western powers.

Socialist Revolutionaries (SRs): A political party that had emerged before the 1905 Revolution. It was an important political party between 1906 and 1917, but was divided into left- and right-wing factions (over economic policies in particular).

Socialist realism: The expression of socialist culture that influenced the arts and literature in particular. It was to contribute to the building of a socialist state under Stalin in the 1930s.

Soviets: Self-elected revolutionary bodies that had first emerged in the 1905 Revolution. They played an important role in the October Revolution.

Sovnarkom: The Russian word for cabinet or government. After March 1918 only Bolsheviks could become members of the Russian government.

State Capitalism: The temporary economic policy of the Bolsheviks from 1917–18. Under this policy the state controlled the economy using its central power and authority.

Stalinism: The political system used to keep Stalin in power by creating a totalitarian dictatorship by 1941.

Triumvirate: Also known by the Russian term *troika*, this political entity was made up of three men – Kamenev, Stalin and Zinoviev – who governed Russia from 1922–25 during Lenin's period of ill health and after his death in January 1924.

Tsarism: A system of government under a tsar; an absolute monarchy.

United Opposition: This was formed in 1926 by Kamenev and Zinoviev, who joined forces with their formal rival Trotsky to oppose Stalin (as he wanted to continue the NEP). Its members were defeated by the end of 1927 and nearly all were killed during the show trials of the 1930s.

USSR: The Union of Soviet Socialist Republics – the new federal system of government created in December 1922.

Vesenkha: The Supreme Council of the National Economy, set up in December 1917.

Whites: The collective name for the different armies that banded together to try and defeat the Reds (Bolsheviks) during the Russian Civil War.

Zhenotdel: The women's department of the Communist Party, formed in 1919 and closed down by the party in 1930.

Bibliography

The books listed below give a good overall view of the period 1914–41. These lists are not comprehensive, but they contain some of the main works relevant to further research on, or as a general introduction to, some of the main topics covered in this book. The first list is of titles that address the whole period; the remainder cover different sections of this book as appropriate.

Recommended Reading

Ascher, Abraham, *Stalin* (Oneworld Publications, 2017)

Brenton, Tony, ed., *Was Revolution Inevitable?: Turning Points of the Russian Revolution* (Oxford University Press, 2017)

Carr, E.H., *The Russian Revolution from Lenin to Stalin, 1917–1929* (Palgrave Macmillan, 2004)

Corin, Chris and Terry Fiehn, *Communist Russia Under Lenin and Stalin* (Hodder Education, 2002)

Evans, David and Jane Jenkins, *Years of Russia and the USSR, 1851–1991* (Hodder Education, 2001)

Figes, Orlando, *A People's Tragedy: Russian Revolution, 1861–1924* (Jonathan Cape, 1996)

——, *Revolutionary Russia, 1891–1991* (Penguin, 2014)

Fitzpatrick, Sheila, *The Russian Revolution* (Oxford University Press, updated ed. 2017)

Hosking, Geoffrey, *A History of the Soviet Union, 1917–1991* (Fontana Press, 1992)

Lynch, Michael, *From Autocracy to Communism, 1894–1941* (Hodder Education, revised ed. 2008)

McCauley, Martin, *The Soviet Union Since 1917* (Longman, 1981)

Oxley, Peter, *Russia 1885–1991: From Tsar to Commissars* (Oxford University Press, 2001)

Rappaport, Helen, *Caught in the Revolution: Petrograd, Russia, 1917 – A World on the Edge* (St. Martin's Press, 2017)

Read, Christopher, *From Tsar To Soviets: Russian People and Their Revolution, 1917–21* (Routledge, 1996)

Sebestyen, Victor, *Lenin the Dictator: An Intimate Portrait* (Weidenfeld & Nicolson, 2017)

Service, Robert, *The Penguin History of Modern Russia: From Tsarism to the Twenty-first Century* (Penguin, updated ed., 2015)

Smith, S.A., *Russia in Revolution: An Empire in Crisis, 1890–1928* (Oxford University Press, 2017)

Stites, Richard, *Russian Popular Culture: Entertainment and Society Since 1900* (Cambridge University Press, 1992)

Swain, Geoffrey, *A Short History of the Russian Revolution* (I.B. Tauris, 2017)

Thomas, David and Mark McAndrew, *Russia Soviet Union 1917–1945: From Tsar to Stalin* (Hodder Education, 1995)

Treadgold, Donald and Herbert J. Ellison, *Twentieth Century Russia* (Westview Press, 2000)

The revolutions of February and October, 1917

Acton, Edward, *Rethinking the Russian Revolution* (Bloomsbury Academic, 1990)

Bainton, Roy, *1917: Russia's Year of Revolution* (Robinson, 2005)

Bushnell, John, 'Peasants in Uniform: The Tsarist Army as a Peasant Society', *Journal of Social History*, Vol. 13, Issue 4 (July 1980)

Darby, Graham, *The Russian Revolution: Tsarism to Bolshevism, 1861–1924* (Longman, 1998)

Figes, Orlando, *A People's Tragedy: A History of the Russian Revolution* (Jonathan Cape, 1996)

——, *Revolutionary Russia, 1891–1991* (Penguin, 2014)

Laver, John, *Personalities & Powers: Lenin – Liberator or Oppressor?* (Hodder Education, 1994)

Merridale, Catherine, *Lenin On The Train* (Penguin, 2016)

Pearson, Michael, *The Sealed Train: Journey to Revolution, Lenin, 1917* (Readers Union, 1975)

Perry, K., *Modern European History* (Made Simple, 1991)

Phillips, Steve, *Lenin and the Russian Revolution* (Heinemann, 2000)

Pipes, Richard, *The Russian Revolution* (Knopf, 1990)

——, *Three Whys of the Russian Revolution* (Pimlico, 1998)

Read, Christopher, *From Tsar To Soviets: Russian People and Their Revolution, 1917–21* (Routledge, 1996)

Reed, John, *Ten Days That Shook the World* (Penguin, 1977)

Sebestyen, Victor, *Lenin the Dictator* (Weidenfeld & Nicolson, 2017)

Service, Robert, *Lenin: A Biography*, (Pan Macmillan, 2011)

——, *The Russian Revolution, 1900–1927* (4th ed., Macmillan, 2009)

Trotsky, Leon, *History of the Russian Revolution* (Penguin, 2017)

Volkogonov, Dmitrii Antonovich, *Lenin: Life And Legacy* (HarperCollins, 1994)

Lenin, 1917–24

Carr, E.H., *The Russian Revolution From Lenin to Stalin, 1917–1929* (new ed., Palgrave Macmillan, 2003)

Chamberlin, William Henry, *The Russian Revolution, Volume II 1918–1921: From the Civil War to the Consolidation of Power* (Princeton University Press, 1987)

Corin, Chris and Terry Fiehn, *Communist Russia Under Lenin and Stalin* (Hodder Education, 2002)

Deutscher, Isaac, *The Prophet Armed: Trotsky 1879–1921* (new ed., Verso, 2003)

Evans, David and Jane Jenkins, *Years of Russia and the USSR, 1851–1991* (Hodder & Stoughton, 2001)

Figes, Orlando, *A People's Tragedy: Russian Revolution, 1891–1924* (Jonathan Cape, 1996)

——, *Revolutionary Russia, 1891–1991: A History* (Penguin, 2014)

Hughes, Gwyneth and Simon Welfare, *Red Empire: The Forbidden History of the USSR* (St Martin's Press, 1991)

Lenin, V.I., *Collected Works, Volume 15* (Lawrence & Wishart, 1963)

——, *Collected Works, Volume 32* (Lawrence & Wishart, 1965)

Lenin, V.I. and Gregory Zinoviev, *Socialism and War* (1915)

Lynch, Michael, *From Autocracy to Communism: Russia 1894–1941* (Hodder, 2008)

——, *Reaction and Revolution: Russia 1894–1924* (4th ed., Hachette, 2015)

McAuley, Mary, *Soviet Politics, 1917–1991* (Oxford University Press, 1992)

Marples, David R., *Lenin's Revolution, Russia 1917–1921* (Pearson Education, 2000)

Mawdsley, Evan, *The Russian Civil War* (Birlinn Ltd, 2008)

Nove, Alec, *An Economic History of the USSR* (Penguin, 1972)

Oxley, Peter, *Russia, 1855–1991: From Tsars to Commissars* (Oxford University Press, 2001)

Phillips, Steve, *Lenin and the Russian Revolution* (Heinemann, 2000)

Pipes, Richard, *Russia Under The Bolshevik Regime, 1919–1924* (Harvill, 1994)

Sebestyen, Victor, *Lenin the Dictator* (Hachette, 2017)

Service, Robert, *A History of Modern Russia from Nicholas II to Vladimir Putin* (Harvard University Press, 2005)

———, *Lenin: A Biography*, (Pan Macmillan, 2011)

———, *The Russian Revolution, 1900–1927* (4th ed., Macmillan, 2009)

———, *Trotsky: A Biography*, (Macmillan, 2009)

Smele, Jonathan D., *The 'Russian' Civil Wars 1916–1926: Ten Years That Shook the World* (Oxford University Press, 2016)

Smith, S.A., *Russia in Revolution 1890–1928*, (Oxford University Press, 2017)

Stites, Richard, *Russian Popular Culture: Entertainment and Society Since 1900* (Cambridge University Press, 1992)

Thomas, David and Mark McAndrew, *Russia/Soviet Union 1917–1945: from Tsar to Stalin* (Hodder Education, 1995)

Trotsky, Leon, *My Life: An Attempt at an Autobiography* (1930)

Wade, Rex A., *The Bolshevik Revolution and the Russian Civil War* (Greenwood Press, 2001)

Stalin, 1924–41

Ascher, Abraham, *Stalin* (Oneworld Publications, 2016)

Bullock, Alan, *Hitler and Stalin, Parallel Lives* (Alfred A. Knopf, 1998)

Butler, Rupert, *Stalin's Secret Police: A History of the CHEKA, OGPU, NKVD, SMERSH & KGB, 1917–1991* (Amber Books, 2017)

Carr, E.H., *The Russian Revolution: From Lenin to Stalin, 1917–1929* (Palgrave Macmillan, 1979)

Conquest, Robert, *The Great Terror: A Reassessment* (Oxford University Press, 2008)

Corin, Chris and Terry Fiehn, *Communist Russia Under Lenin and Stalin* (Hodder Education, 2002)

Cuplin, Chris and Jim Grant, *Stalin and the Soviet Union* (Longman, 1998)

Davies, Sarah and James Harris, *Stalin: A New History* (Cambridge University Press, 2005)

Deutscher, Isaac, *The Prophet Unarmed: Leon Trotsky, 1921–1929* (new ed., Verso, 2003)

——, *Stalin: A Political Biography* (Penguin, 1990)

Evans, David, *Understand Stalin's Russia* (Hachette, 2012)

Figes, Orlando, *Revolutionary Russia, 1891–1991* (Penguin, 2014)

——, *The Whisperers: Private Life in Stalin's Russia* (Penguin, 2008)

Fitzpatrick, Sheila, *The Cultural Front: Power and Culture in Revolutionary Russia* (Cornell University Press, 2010)

Fitzpatrick, Sheila, *Everyday Stalinism: Ordinary Life in Extraordinary Times: Soviet Russia in the 1930s* (Oxford University Press, 1999)

——, *The Russian Revolution* (Oxford University Press, 1994)

Gill, Graeme, *Stalinism* (Palgrave, 1998)

Ili, Melanie (ed), *Women in the Stalin Era. Studies in Russian and East European History and Society* (Palgrave Macmillan, 2001)

Kishlansky, Mark A., Patrick J. Geary, Patricia O'Brien, *Civilization in the West, Volume 2* (Longman, 2003)

Kotkin, Stephen, *Magnetic Mountain: Stalinism as a Civilization* (University of California Press, 1997)

——, *Stalin: Paradoxes of Power, 1878–1928* (Penguin, 2015)

Laver, John, *The Impact of Stalin's Leadership in the USSR, 1924–1941* (Oxford University Press, 2008)

——, *Joseph Stalin – From Revolutionary to Despot* (Hodder, 1993)

Lee, Stephen J., *Europe, 1890–1945* (Routledge, 2003)

——, *European Dictatorships, 1918–1945* (4th ed. Routledge, 2016)

——, *Stalin and the Soviet Union* (Routledge, 1999)

Lenin, V.I., *Collected Works, Volume 36* (Lawrence & Wishart, 1966)

Lynch, Michael, *Access to History: From Autocracy to Communism, 1894–1941* (Hodder, 2008)

——, *Access to History: Russia 1894–1941* (Hodder, 2015)

McCauley, Martin, *The Rise and Fall of the Soviet Union* (Routledge, 2013)

——, *Stalin and Stalinism* (3rd ed. Routledge, 2013)

Medvedev, Roy, *Let History Judge: The Origins and Consequences of Stalinism* (new ed., Columbia University Press, 1990)

Montefiore, Simon Sebag, *Stalin: The Court of the Red Tsar* (Weidenfeld & Nicolson, 2014)

——, *Young Stalin* (Weidenfeld & Nicolson, 2008)

North, David, *In Defense of Leon Trotsky* (Mehring Books, 2010)

Nove, Alec, *An Economic History of the USSR 1917–1991* (Penguin, 1972)

Peris, Daniel, *Storming the Heavens: The Soviet League of the Militant Godless* (Cornell University Press, 1998)

Phillips, Steve, *Stalinist Russia* (Heinemann, 2000)

Plamper, Jan, *The Stalin Cult: A Study in the Alchemy of Power* (Yale University Press, 2012)

Radzinsky, Edvard, *Stalin: The First In-Depth Biography Based on Explosive New Documents from Russia's Secret Archives* (Anchor Books, 1997)

Rappaport, Helen, *Joseph Stalin: A Biographical Companion*, (ABC CLIO, 1999)

Rayfield, Donald, *Stalin and His Hangmen: An Authoritative Portrait of a Tyrant and Those Who Served Him* (Penguin, 2005)

Reed, John, *Ten Days That Shook the World* (Penguin, 1977)

Rigby, Thomas Henry, *Stalin* (Prentice-Hall, 1966)

Schapiro, Leonard, *Communist Party of the Soviet Union* (Eyre & Spottiswoode, 1960)

Service, Robert, *Comrades!: A History of World Communism* (Harvard University Press, 2007)

————, *Stalin: A Biography* (Macmillan, 2010)

————, *Trotsky: A Biography* (Macmillan, 2009)

Stites, Richard, *Russian Popular Culture: Entertainment and Society Since 1900* (Cambridge University Press, 1992)

Thomas, David and Mark McAndrew, *Russia/Soviet Union 1917–1945: from Tsar to Stalin* (Hodder Education, 1995)

Trotsky, Leon and Wright, John G. (trans.) 'The Lessons of October', *Collected Works, Volume 3* (Pioneer Publishers, 1937)

Tumarkin, Nina, *Lenin Lives!: The Lenin Cult in Soviet Russia* (Harvard University Press, 1997)

Volkogonov, Dmitri and Harold Shukman (ed. and trans.), *Stalin: Triumph and Tragedy* (Weidenfeld & Nicolson, 1991)

Volkogonov, Dmitri, *Trotsky: The Eternal Revolutionary* (HarperCollins, 2008)

Ward, Chris, *Stalin's Russia* (2nd ed., Bloomsbury Academic, 1999)

Welch, David, *Modern European History 1871–2000* (Routledge, 2003)

Whittock, Martyn, *Stalin's Russia* (HarperCollins, 1997)

Copyright Information

The author and publisher gratefully acknowledge permission to include the following copyright images:

Front cover 'Vladimir Lenin and Joseph Stalin arrive at Finland station, Petrograd', DK0814, ©Tate Images

p.17 'A crowd outside the Duma in Petrograd,1917', ©Imperial War Museum (Q 69399)

p.19 'Tsar Nicholas II of Russia with troops', DRK0RB, Chronicle / Alamy Stock Photo

p.31 'People queue for food, Moscow,1917', EK35BG, ITAR-TASS News Agency / Alamy Stock Photo

p.33 'Government troops firing on demonstrators', KC7P.8X, Artokoloro Quint Lox Limited / Alamy Stock Photo

p.34 'Soldiers of tsarist army at their positions', B9PDWR, SPUTNIK / Alamy Stock Photo

p.59 'Lenin addressing a crowd of soldiers', FBWWF8, IanDagnall Computing / Alamy Stock Photo

p.62 'Leon Trotsky reviewing Red Army troops' DK0809, ©Tate Images

p.82 'Lenin with his wife Nadezhda Krupskaya, 1922', HMRHK0, Pictorial Press Ltd / Alamy Stock Photo

p.97 'An agitprop train during the Russian Civil War', DK0152, ©Tate Images

p.119 'Trotsky during a party meeting, 1923', GG2F46, Photo 12 / Alamy Stock Photo

p.134 'Sergey Kirov's funeral, December 6, 1934', DE8G7T, Heritage Image Partnership Ltd / Alamy Stock Photo

p.138 'Josef Stalin making notes', DK0436, ©Tate Images

p.142 'French poster showing Lenin's General Staff' DK0810, ©Tate Images

p.171 'Peasant demonstration in Russia', DK0811, ©Tate Images

p.179 '10 Niet poster promoting the Five-Year Plan' by A. Vedeneev, DK0812, ©Tate Images

p.194 'Poster of 17th Congress Communist Party', GG2BMF, Photo 12 / Alamy Stock Photo

p.197 'Labourers forced to work on the Stalin-Belomor Canal', DK0387, ©Tate Images

Copyright has been acknowledged to the best of our ability. If there are any inadvertent errors or omissions, we shall be happy to correct them in any future editions.

Examination Guidance

The examination questions for CCEA AS History Unit 2, Option 5: Russia 1914–41 address two different types of historical skills, with each question being divided into two separate parts that must be completed together. Students have 90 minutes to answer two complete questions from a choice of three. Each question is broken down into two further parts – a short (8 mark) and long (22 mark) response. This gives students 45 minutes in total for each complete question selected. Candidates should spend about 10 minutes on the 8-mark (short response) question and about 30 minutes on the 22-mark (mini-essay) question. Good time management and a strong focus, using relevant knowledge to address the question selected, can help students achieve good marks for their responses to each question.

In this unit, there are no source-based questions and an awareness of historiography is also not assessed. The best responses to examination questions are well organised with selective use of relevant historical knowledge to show understanding of the topic being discussed. Weaker responses tend to contain common errors or demonstrate flaws that prevent candidates from achieving top-level marks. These responses may ignore the focus of the question – for example, discussing economic problems rather than political problems; or only examining Lenin's role in the October Revolution and overlooking Trotsky – or they may ignore the dates given in the question – for instance, a lengthy digression on the period 1894–1914 when the question called for an analysis of the period 1914–17. These digressions are irrelevant and attract no marks as the content is not helpful.

A wealth of useful information – including specimen papers, past papers and mark schemes, for both the 8-mark and 22-mark questions – is available on the CCEA History microsite. Students are strongly advised to make use of this valuable resource: www.rewardinglearning.org.uk/microsites/history/

How to answer the 8-mark question

The 8-mark question is a short response that assesses historical knowledge and understanding, but that does not require historical analysis or argument. For instance, candidates could be asked to explain the causes, features, aims or consequences of a leader, government, policy or key historical event (these are illustrative examples only – there are many different types of 8-mark questions that may come up in the examination).

The best answers to the 8-mark question identify and explain the importance of four to five main points relevant to the question selected. There is no need for an introduction or conclusion, as candidates will only have about 10 minutes to answer in practice tests and examinations. Candidates should avoid generalisations, digressions and the use of historically inaccurate or irrelevant evidence to ensure that examination time is not wasted. Frequent practice of this type of question under exam-type conditions and timing is recommended.

How to answer the 22-mark question

The 22-mark question is a longer response in the form of a mini-essay that assesses historical knowledge and understanding. These questions assess a candidate's skill at understanding topics in history and their ability to use the information presented in an analytical form with a clear line of argument. To do this, answers must be well organised and use appropriate historical material in a logical and coherent manner.

In the 22-mark question, candidates are presented with a proposition about an important area of Russian history. This can be presented through a structured question or the use of an historical quotation where candidates are asked if they agree or disagree with the selected statement. Good preparation and regular practice in answering this type of question will help students improve their historical skills and technique.

Candidates must learn to deconstruct this type of question, which can usually be divided into three different parts:

1. The instruction – for example, 'how far', 'to what extent' and so on.
2. The topic – for example, the civil war, collectivisation and so on.
3. The key words – for example, 'the key factor', 'the most important' and so on.

Use this method for the sample question given below. This is just an illustrative example of the type of 22-mark question used in the examination for this unit:

"Trotsky's leadership was the most important reason for Bolshevik victory in the Russian Civil War by 1921." How far would you accept this verdict?

1. The instruction – **How far?**
2. The topic – **The civil war and Trotsky**
3. The key words – **The most important reason**

One of the most common reasons for underperforming in exams is the failure to produce a relevant answer so candidates should spend a few minutes planning and organising the response, then spend about 30 minutes writing the mini-essay. The best answers to this type of question will constantly engage with the question itself and present clear judgements, with a strong focus on the proposition and the topic being assessed. Candidates should avoid generalisations, digressions and the use of historically inaccurate or irrelevant evidence. Students should also avoid producing a narrative of events or a mini biography of a key figure, which fails to address and engage with the question.

Frequent practice of this type of question under exam conditions and timing – including practice in deconstructing the question – is recommended. Students should also carefully prepare their revision notes, ideally using past papers and mark schemes – a common reason for underperformance in examinations is the lack of adequate revision of the main topics covered. Finally, to improve chances of success, students should read exam questions carefully to ensure that their answers are relevant, clear and accurate.

Index